Personality

Personality

WHAT MAKES YOU THE WAY YOU ARE

DANIEL NETTLE

OXFORD
UNIVERSITY PRESS

OXFORD

UNIVERSITY PRESS

Great Clarendon Street, Oxford OX2 6DP

Oxford University Press is a department of the University of Oxford.
It furthers the University's objective of excellence in research, scholarship,
and education by publishing worldwide in

Oxford New York

Auckland Cape Town Dar es Salaam Hong Kong Karachi
Kuala Lumpur Madrid Melbourne Mexico City Nairobi
New Delhi Shanghai Taipei Toronto

With offices in

Argentina Austria Brazil Chile Czech Republic France Greece
Guatemala Hungary Italy Japan Poland Portugal Singapore
South Korea Switzerland Thailand Turkey Ukraine Vietnam

Oxford is a registered trade mark of Oxford University Press
in the UK and in certain other countries

Published in the United States
by Oxford University Press Inc., New York

British Library Cataloguing in Publication Data

Data available

Library of Congress Cataloging in Publication Data

Data available

Typeset by SPI Publisher Services, Pondicherry, India
Printed in Great Britain
on acid-free paper by
CPI Mackays Ltd., Chatham

ISBN 978–0–19–921142–5

1 3 5 7 9 10 8 6 4 2

Contents

At every single moment of one's life one is what
one is going to be no less than what one has been.

Oscar Wilde, *De Profundis*

Introduction

I do not plead guilty to a shallow view of human nature, when I propose to apply, as it were, a foot-rule to its heights and depths.

Francis Galton

Lee is a successful, smart, business executive, rising 35 and rising through the ranks at the same time. He is considered effective and dynamic at work. In fact, it's more than that. He does not suffer fools gladly, and if he thinks colleagues or suppliers are trying to pull one over on him, he is quick to speak his mind. He can be very cutting, and fly into a deep rage, during which he will tell people what he thinks of them and their behaviour without sparing their blushes. As a result, though he is good at what he does, he builds up enemies. He has moved firms a few times, or had to be moved between departments, because he gets into feuds and stand-offs. Some more conciliatory colleague will have to step in to calm the waters, or simply to ensure that Lee and his latest enemy don't have to deal with each other.

Outside of work, there are quite a lot of people Lee doesn't like. He has been to a fair few exotic countries, and for at least some of these, he has decided that he hates the natives. They are too rude, or too slow, or invade his personal space. He hates people who cut him up on the road, or barge in front of him in line, or make him wait. He is quick to get angry when this happens, and not averse to a muttered, usually scatological, insult. We should not assume that Lee doesn't like to socialize. In fact, he loves to go out and party. However, if the people at the party are the wrong type of people, or they are partying in the wrong way, he is quickly bored and frankly annoyed at having wasted his evening. Even a good party might end up with Lee in a screaming row with some fool who doesn't share his politics or tastes.

Lee has a core of good friends, and these friendships have lasted, but they are not without conflict. In fact, in each, there is a history of strong arguments, altercations, and sulks, as well as reconciliations. Love is a similar story. There always seem to be disagreements, or the other person turns out to be needy, annoying, or inadequate in some way. Women tend to end up saying Lee is selfish, or inconsiderate, and a partner who is compatible for the long haul is still not in sight.

Julian is very different from Lee. He is (currently) a writer for a travel magazine. This job allows him to travel all over the world, researching stories on Indian religious festivals and the Trans-Siberian Railway. Travel is his current passion, though it was not always so. He studied music at college, and immediately after graduation threw himself with passion into his band, which performed an unusual combination of traditional Middle Eastern music and modern pop. Guided mainly by his motivating enthusiasm, the band did quite well in their region for a few years, though doing quite well in the music business is not as glamorous as it might seem. It means playing live, a lot, but to maybe thirty or fifty people, and sleeping in vans and sharing flats with numerous others of uncertain hygiene. These costs are not to be questioned, though, since music is clearly everything.

A couple of years into the life of the band, Julian began to become disillusioned, and for a period became low and withdrawn. He felt that his life with his partner, one of the band's Lebanese backing singers, was becoming repetitive and joyless, and he worried about what would happen to them in the end. What had previously seemed incredibly exciting flipped into seeming like a treadmill on which they would never get anywhere. Julian eventually left both the band and his partner and, much to the surprise of his friends, enrolled in a Master's degree in business management. Julian, the rock and roller, in a business suit? Julian would have none of it. Business is *really* interesting. It's about people, it's about how they interact. In fact, it's *creative*. It's a way of bringing about new relationships and better ways of living.

Needless to say, that didn't last. By the time of graduation, Julian could only see the entrapment of thirty years of 9-to-5 working in an office ahead of him. This time he became really depressed, and saw both a doctor, who prescribed antidepressants, and a counsellor, who introduced him to some of the more New Age elements of psychotherapy. For a while he made his living, with his then girlfriend, doing Reiki, psychodrama, and Indian head massage, the two of them living frugally but healthily in a large rambling farmhouse in a remote spot. They didn't need foreign holidays, so vivifying and healthy was the way they lived all year around.

That lasted three years, until a rift with his partner, and disillusion with the therapies he was practising, led Julian into his glummest spirits yet. He resolved to travel the world for a year, to revitalize himself, and through a series of chance encounters, ended up writing features for the travel magazine. He loves his job—he has been doing it for a year—and has a fabulous French girlfriend, who is a photographer. Clearly, travelling and travel writing is what he has always been working towards.

Their lives are so different, Lee and Julian, and yet they are the same age and sex. We can easily imagine them both coming from fairly normal middle-class backgrounds, being of similar intelligence and educational attainment, and having been exposed to broadly similar cultural expectations and values. In fact, it is no stretch of the imagination, given our experience of human beings, to imagine two people having essentially the same set of experiences growing up, and yet having adult lives at least as different from each other as those of Lee and Julian. If the initial social conditions were so similar, then what could possibly account for two human lives coming out so differently?

Non-psychologists I talk to have strong intuitions about this question. What brings about the different outcomes is, they say, the different personalities, or temperaments, or characters, of the two individuals involved. What is personality, I ask? They tell me that it is something internal, stable, inherent to the person, something which stands in a causal relationship to their specific choices, motivations, reactions, and obstacles when faced with the stream of events. A clue to personality being at work, they tell me, is a kind of thematic recurrence within the events of a life. For example, over the course of a few years, Lee eventually ends up hostile about most of the people he has to work with. In the same way, he is quite likely to end up being hostile about someone he has to sit next to on a train journey or flight. The timescale is quite different, and the stakes and demands of the interaction are very different, but the fact that, sooner or later, another person in close proximity is likely to do something to annoy him, recurs as a *leitmotif* across Lee's life. (A *leitmotif* I suspect Lee will never consider, since he finds psychologists and psychology books really annoying.)

Similarly for Julian, there are a number of recurring patterns. Each of the domains of fusion music, psychodrama, self-sufficient farm living, and travel writing is unusual and creative, but Julian has been drawn to them all within a short life. It is as if there is a constant quest for new ways of experiencing the world and expressing his experience of it. There is also a characteristic pattern to his life choices. He finds a new domain and becomes tremendously, infectiously excited and activated by it. This serves him very well in getting his new projects established. For a while, he simply will not hear of the drawbacks or limitations. Over time, though, these feelings fade, and in place of enthusiasm come doubt and worry about the future, for despite his energy, Julian can be a very worried and sad person.

The pattern that describes Julian's career activities also describes his relationships. These have typically lasted two or three years, and consisted of an initial phase of great passion, during which his family's mild suggestions of unsuitability are just *so* ridiculous, unintuitive, and superficial, followed by a period of mounting unhappiness, restlessness, and withdrawal, during which his family's resigned attempts to get on with his chosen paramour are resented. ('How can they not see that she is not what I need?' It is the lot of parents to always be in the wrong.) This phase is followed by a period of more or less nervy adjustment and recuperation, before the next passion takes hold.

Can this *leitmotif* of initial enthusiasm, followed by withdrawal and denial, be detected at any other level? As I imagine him, Julian has dozens of unopened books that he brought home from the book shop with a triumphant 'Nietzsche is *so* interesting. I am going to read everything he ever wrote'. There is a bread maker, bought in a flurry of excitement but used twice, a violin, played once, and a full-sized loom(!) Each of these items represents a spurt of enthusiasm and a desire to begin something unusual, followed by either insufficient reward to sustain the behaviour, or a slough of demotivating negative emotion. This is the same pattern as the relationships and jobs, but over a different scale.

The same pattern appearing at different scales is a very interesting property. It is, for example, a property of those exquisite topographies called fractals much beloved of complexity theorists and graphic designers. In a fractal, you see the same pattern whether you look at a very large section or whether you zoom in on a very small one. The part represents the whole, and vice versa. Fractals have this property because of the nature of the mathematical functions that generate them.

Human personalities are rather like fractals. It is not just that what we do in the large-scale narratives of our lives—love, career, friendships—tends to be somewhat consistent over time, with us often repeating the same kinds of triumphs or mistakes. Rather, what we do in tiny interactions like the way we shop, or dress, or talk to a stranger on a train, or decorate our houses, shows the same kinds of patterns as can be observed from examining a whole life. We often find ourselves saying, 'That is just so typical of Bob . . .'. We say this because what people do in the set of situations we have observed them in is a reasonable guide to what they will do in a set of future situations, including quite different ones. Just as the self-consistent properties of fractals are generated by the mathematical functions that define them, so the self-consistent properties of personality seem as if they are generated by some physical property of the nervous system of the person in question. In other words, we feel that talking about someone's personality is a shorthand way for talking about the way that person's particular nervous system is wired up.[1]

This book is about the psychology of personality. I aim to vindicate the idea that people have enduring personality dispositions which partly predict what they will do, and which stem from the way their nervous systems are wired up. I also wish to introduce the science behind the study of personality—how we measure personality, what the measures mean, what they predict, and why personality variation exists in the first place. Personality psychology has, until recently, had a rather low status compared to other branches of psychology. It has been perceived as based on flimsy evidence, internally divided, and far removed from the 'hard science' end of psychology. There may once have been some justice in these views, but I believe that things have changed. In fact, a renaissance is underway in the study of personality, a renaissance I hope to herald in this book.

There are several reasons why the time is right for the renaissance. First, we at last have a set of personality concepts we can use that is firmly based on evidence, and which we psychologists can agree on. This set of concepts is called the five-factor model of personality, or the big five. The five-factor model has emerged from a welter of research over the last few decades and looks to be the most comprehensive, reliable and useful framework for discussing human personality that we have ever had (Chapter 1). The idea of the model is that there are five major dimensions along which all human characters vary. Thus, any individual can be given five scores that will tell us a great deal about the ways they are liable to behave through their lives.

The emergence of the five-factor model is very useful, because the field of personality research had long been plagued by different people using different notions. Formerly, one psychologist might give you a score for Reward Dependence and Harm Avoidance, whilst another might classify you as a Thinking, Feeling, Sensing, or Intuiting type. This led to a frustrating profusion of different studies measuring different constructs without seeming to relate to each other in any systematic way. All this added to the low status of personality research as a scientific endeavour. As long ago as 1958, Gordon Allport complained that 'each assessor has his own pet units and uses a pet battery of diagnostic devices', and things got worse in the ensuing decades.[2]

The five-factor model introduced some order into the mess. It's not that all those other constructs were necessarily invalid. It's just that most constructs that had previously been measured can actually be subsumed under the five-factor framework—either they measure one of the big five, or a sub-part of one of them, or an amalgam of two of them. This is enormously useful, as we can quickly tidy the field up very significantly, and give people a fully portable framework for understanding and characterizing the main differences between people. To quote the influential personality psychologists Paul Costa and Robert McCrae, the five-factor model is the 'Christmas tree' on which all the particular findings of personality research can be arranged. I am using the five-factor model as my Christmas tree in this book too: each one of the big five is the subject of one chapter (Chapters 3 to 7 inclusive).[3]

Another reason that we are ready for a renaissance of personality studies is the staggering progress of neuroscience, fuelled in particular by brain-imaging techniques such as PET scanning and fMRI, which we will meet frequently later in the book. These techniques allow us to look at the structure and functioning of the human brain non-invasively in alive, awake, thinking individuals. The first flurry of activity using these new technologies was about finding out how brains *in general* worked—which regions were always associated with which types of functions—but a second phase has become concerned with the variation between individuals. Different brain structures have different relative sizes within the 'normal' population, and there is a great deal of variation between individuals in the way their brains respond metabolically to particular tasks. A new science is emerging of individual differences in brain structure and functioning, and the results of this science can be mapped back to the big five personality dimensions, as we shall see.

The third area contributing to the renaissance of interest in personality is human genetics and genomics. The sequencing of the human genome was completed in 2001. Just as in brain imaging, the first concern was understanding people in general, not as individuals. The initial goal of the human genome project was thus to describe the common structure of the 25–30,000 genes that we all share, and was based on a 'consensus' sequence of around two hundred individuals' DNA. The consensus sequence has now been published, and there is a growing interest in genetic individuality. Many of those 25–30,000 genes exist in several slightly different variant forms. We know that people vary enormously in disease liabilities, response to particular drugs, vulnerability to specific types of psychological problems, and many other ways, and we are beginning to understand how these predispositions relate to which of the possible genetic variants they are carrying. We all know our blood group, and, in the not too distant future, we can envisage a world in which we will get our personal genome sequenced, in order to know our vulnerability to breast cancer or heart disease, or likely response to a particular type of drug. This burgeoning science of genetic individuality can also be linked back to personality, since, as we shall see, your personality is partly determined by which genetic variants you are carrying.

The final reason why the time is right for a personality renaissance is to do with the diffusion of evolutionary thinking. Evolutionary thinking is about asking the ultimate question of how the population got to be the way it is through natural selection, alongside the proximate question of which genes or bits of brain are involved. Evolutionary thinking is becoming much more widespread in psychology, and it is lending a new depth and explanatory power to several different areas of the field. Just as in the other areas of science discussed above, the initial concern of evolutionary psychologists was with understanding the design of the mental mechanisms we all share, and so at first, they gave relatively little thought to differences between individuals. Only a few small forays of evolutionary thought into the psychology of personality were made. However, that is also changing. We know that there are temperamental differences between individuals in species other than humans. An evolutionary perspective on such variation raises a host of good questions. Why is the variation there? Will natural selection ultimately eliminate it, or lead to its increase? Under what circumstances, indeed, does natural selection allow variation to persist within a population? These questions will infuse our thinking about personality traits throughout this book.[4]

This book is aimed at the interested general reader, rather than just my academic colleagues. In this spirit, I will not dwell on the kinds of technical details and full background to every claim that would normally be found in a research paper or monograph. Those wishing to find citations and ancillary details are directed to the endnotes, though even these offer pointers and key references rather than a complete literature review. Those who can live without the academic stuff should be able to ignore the notes completely without missing anything vital to the argument. Even in this (hopefully) user-friendly presentation, I will try to give a judicious and evidence-based account of current knowledge, and be fair in separating what we know from what is as yet guesswork. My account is based on several elements: the existing literature, created by many esteemed colleagues; some recent personality studies of my own; and a remarkable set of life stories sent to me by correspondents from all over the world. These were individuals who had been participants in my research, and for whom I thus had five-factor personality data. At my request, they kindly wrote to me—often at length—about their lives, their feelings, and their relationships with others in ways that have been most enlightening, even if they have sometimes made writing this book harder, rather than easier, since they make the picture more complex. Where I draw on their stories, I have of course disguised details to ensure their anonymity. (By the way, Lee and Julian are not examples of these life stories. They are the only fictional case studies in this book. The rest are drawn from life.)

I solicited the life stories because I suspected that most readers of this book were more interested in understanding people than in understanding personality theory for theory's sake. Above all, if you are reading this, I suspect you want to know about and understand your own personality. I would therefore urge you to turn to the Appendix and score yourself using the Newcastle Personality Assessor before we go any further and you know too much about what is riding on your answers. You may like to have your scores to hand as you read the subsequent chapters, especially Chapters 3 to 7, where we meet the big five one by one. Before we can meet them, though, we have to explore a couple of preliminary but vital issues: first, in Chapter 1, what is a personality trait; and then, in Chapter 2, why does evolution allow biological differences between individuals of the same species to persist?

I

Character Matters

Personality is and does something... It is what lies behind specific acts and within the individual.

Gordon Allport

It might be conventional to begin with Hippocrates, and his ideas about the four humours, or with some other ancient conception of personality types. I prefer, however, to begin our story with an article published by Sir Francis Galton in *The Fortnightly Review* for 1884 entitled 'The Measurement of Character'. Galton is an apt place to begin for a number of reasons. As Charles Darwin's first cousin, Galton was an early champion of evolution and of the view that evolution is relevant to humans. The way he could think of applying it was filtered through his Victorian preconceptions about society and societies, and so does not seem appropriate to us today. However, his basic intuition that the theory of natural selection would ultimately have to inform our thinking about everything people do has turned out to be correct.[1]

A second reason for interest in Galton is that it was he who first realized that studies of how characteristics ran in families, and particularly studies of twins, were the key to unlocking the contribution of nature and nurture to human variation. This insight lies behind a whole scientific field, known as behaviour genetics, a field that has flourished since Galton's time, and whose results we will meet later on.

Finally, Galton is noteworthy because he had a very modern preoccupation with measurement. Galton was obsessed with trying to find practical measures for obscure bits of human behaviour. In 1885, he published a paper in *Nature* entitled 'The Measurement of Fidget'. In this he notes, from his own extensive observations, that in a large gathering such as a lecture, audience members fidget around once a minute on average. However, when the lecturer really holds their attention with a point, this rate is diminished by around a half, and moreover, the fidgeting changes. The period of the movements reduces (an enthralled audience member gets their movement over as quickly as possible, whereas a bored one draws it out), and the angle of deviation of the body from the upright (which sailors will know as the 'yaw') also reduces. Thus a quick index of how bored an audience is at any point in time would be on average how far from vertically upright they were. Galton commends these insights to the reader as promising to give 'numerical expression to the amount of boredom expressed by the audience generally during the reading of any particular memoir'.[2]

Quirky as this paper is, it is very modern. Many philosophers before Galton had speculated about human traits, but few had seen that none of this was worth the candle—scientifically at any rate—if the traits in question could not be measured. Most of the work in scientific psychology consists in trying to come up with good measures of things, and showing that they are good measures. Indeed, a concern with measurement is precisely what distinguishes 'academically respectable' psychology from psychology of other kinds. Galton measured the weights of livestock and aristocrats, the speeds of reaction times, the sizes of heads, the shapes of fingerprints, and many other characteristics. His special contribution to personality theory was that he began to think about how this thing—personality—might be measured, and thus brought within the fold of scientifically studiable entities.

In his 1884 article, he notes the general desirability of measuring personality, and comes up with some suggestions. One is that we look at natural language. Using a thesaurus, he estimates that there are at least 1000 terms describing people's characters in the English language, but these contain a good deal of redundancy, since many of them are synonyms or antonyms. This casual observation of Galton's began what is known as lexical work in personality, which analyses the set of descriptive terms occurring in languages as a basis for understanding the ways in which people differ. The assumption is that the semantics of natural language has developed in such a way as to mirror the important differences that exist in the world. I have little more to say about lexical work here, but it has been very important indeed in the development of the five-factor model in particular.[3]

Galton also proposes that people have characteristically different levels of emotional reactivity—again a notion that has turned out to have some mileage in it—and suggests that we could get an index of character by subjecting people to small impromptu emotional trials, to see how they respond (boo!) The magnitude of their response would tell us about the arousability of their emotions in general, which would be predictively useful when thinking about larger trials they might face in real life. Sir Francis is characteristically bullish about how easy this would be to do. 'I feel sure that if two or three experimenters were to act zealously and judiciously as secret accomplices, they would soon collect abundant statistics of conduct.' I feel sure they would, too, but I am less sure that research ethics committees would be pleased.

Finally, Galton notes the desirability of linking these reactions to physiology. If some people are more emotionally arousable than others, then this should show up in changes in heart rate or some other physiological parameters. There were technical limitations to doing this in 1884, but again, it is a very modern idea which prefigures the contemporary interest in linking personality constructs to underlying neurobiological mechanisms. Thus, Galton has already envisioned, at least in principle, many of the methods of modern personality psychology. What is missing from his account is the most common source of personality data today, namely ratings. Much modern personality work is based on people's self-reported ratings of what they are like, or, more rarely, of what someone else is like. It is a fortunate development for personality psychology that data of this kind have turned out to be quite reliable, since they are the quickest and easiest of data to collect.

Systematic empirical work on personality began a few decades after Galton, but this is not the place for a history of personality psychology. Suffice it to say for current purposes that the central notion of personality psychology is the *trait*. A trait is a continuum along which individuals vary. Nervousness might be a trait, for example, or speed of reaction. (Note, at this point, that the same name is often used for one end of a trait, and for the trait itself. Thus, the trait of nervousness means the continuum from 'never at all nervous' to 'often severely nervous'. Similarly, the trait of Extraversion means the continuum from 'Not at all extraverted' to 'Extremely extraverted').[4]

You can never observe a trait directly. Instead, you infer a person's level of the trait through their behaviour. No-one

will be nervous all the time, but some people might be nervous more often and over a wider range of circumstances
than others. This propensity to nervousness, to qualify as a
trait, would have to be fairly consistent over time. (By the
way, the big five are traits. I think people call it the five-
factor rather than the five-trait model because they like the
alliteration.)

Traits are continuous, like height is, rather than discrete,
like being an apple versus being a pear. The idea that there
is some finite number of discrete 'types' of human character is enduringly popular in some quarters, but there is
no basis to it. The architecture of traits is the same across
persons, and their levels alone differ. That is, everyone has
all of the five factors of personality, just as everyone has a
height and a weight. Where we differ is the magnitude of
the height and the weight, or the score along each of the five
dimensions.[5]

Though trait concepts are not derived from neurobiological evidence, many personality psychologists believe that
they will turn out to be neurobiologically real. That is to
say, although we initially define traits by inferring them from
the mass of behaviour, if we had perfect knowledge of the
structure of the nervous system, 'Bob is high in Neuroticism'
could ultimately be translated into statements about the
structure of his brain. Thus trait statements entail predictions
about neurobiological and perhaps even genetic differences

between people. These are the central tenets of modern personality psychology.

Let us then investigate how personality traits are detected and understood. We will do so using some data from a recent study of mine. I asked 545 British adults, of a cross-section of ages and backgrounds, various questions about themselves, which they had to respond to on scales of 1 to 5. One question asked:

How much time do you spend in social activities?

whilst another asked:

How much do you like to travel?[6]

The correlation between people's ratings of how much time they spend in social activities and how much they like to travel is 0.20. You will recall that a correlation coefficient (known as r) is an index of the extent to which, when one quantity varies, some other quantity varies too. A correlation coefficient of 1 means that varying the first quantity perfectly predicts the way the second will vary. A correlation coefficient of 0 means that when one quantity varies, it gives you no information about the other. A person's height and their weight correlate at about $r = 0.68$. This is an index of the fact that if someone is extremely tall, they will probably be relatively heavy, whereas if they are quite small, they will probably be light too. The correlation is not equal to 1 because height and weight do not perfectly predict each other, since two people of the same height can have considerably different weights. Nonetheless, the correlation is substantially greater than zero, which means that if you had to guess how heavy someone was, knowing their height would put you in a better position than if you did not know it.

The correlation in my data between liking for travel and time spent in social activities is much lower than that between height and weight, but still significantly greater than zero. This is interesting, since there is little *logical* connection between the two. A person could love to travel in a solitary manner, whilst generally avoiding social company, but that is not the general trend amongst these 545 people. I also asked the people how competitive they were (in their own opinion). The correlation between competitiveness and liking for travel was 0.12, and that between competitiveness and time spent in social activities was 0.11. These are modest, but significantly greater than zero. Now this starts to be interesting. You might imagine that competitive people are so driven that they have no time for travel or socializing, but that is not what the data show; those who love to socialize and travel also get energized by competition (on average, with a lot of idiosyncratic variation, of course).

Next, I asked people how interested they were in sex. Now we have more correlation coefficients to display, and so we need a table (Table 1). Interest in sex turns out to be significantly, though modestly, correlated with all the other three.

Table 1. Correlations between four rating variables in 545 British adults. All correlations are significantly greater than zero.

	Social	Travel	Compet.	Sex
Social activities	1	0.20	0.11	0.25
Travel		1	0.12	0.16
Competitiveness			1	0.18
Interest in sex				1

On average, someone who likes to travel will also be a bit more competitive, a bit more interested in sex, and likely to spend a bit more time in social activities, than someone who does not like to travel so much. Another way of expressing this is that there is a certain amount of redundancy in the data. If we know someone is really interested in sex, it is not going to surprise us much if they turn out to be a live-hard, play-hard type who loves foreign holidays. The attitude towards sex carries some information about the other attributes, not perfect information by any means, but some information nonetheless.

Now let us introduce some more variables. I also asked people to report whether they had ever sought help, informal or professional, because they were feeling 'down' or 'blue', and, in another question, whether they had sought help because of how anxious or worried they were feeling. Help for feeling blue and help for feeling anxious were positively correlated with each other: $r = 0.46$. This means someone who had sought serious help for anxiety was more likely than average to have also sought serious help for feeling down. The two tend to occur in the same people.

This is not perhaps terribly surprising, but what is more interesting is the relationship of these two to the variables we have already introduced. You might make hypotheses either way. You could suppose that people who are getting out there, socializing hard, driving themselves hard, and having eventful personal lives are going to be exposing themselves to the risk of depression and burnout, and so there will be possible correlations between these two new variables and competitiveness, travel, and so on. On the hand, you could make the opposite prediction. People who are travelling, socializing, etc. are obviously cheerful and resilient types, so there is going to be a negative correlation between these behaviours and depression and anxiety. This would mean that the higher the score on the travelling and socializing variables, the lower the score on the depression and anxiety variables, and it would mean r was less than zero, and some-where towards -1, which is a perfect negative correlation.

In fact, none of the correlations between the depression variable and travel, competitiveness, social activity, or interest in sex is significantly different from zero. The same is true for the anxiety variable. If you want to know if someone is vulnerable to depression or anxiety, then knowing if they love to travel or are very interested in sex gives you absolutely no information either way. Whatever determines vulnerability to these conditions is simply unrelated to whatever makes some people more competitive or sexual than others.

A problem we soon encounter in this type of work is that the number of correlation coefficients we need to calculate rises exponentially with the number of variables we wish to consider. With two variables, we need to calculate one correlation; with three variables, three correlations; with four variables, six correlations; with five variables, ten correlations; with ten variables, forty-six correlations; and so on. This is tedious and makes it more and more difficult to apprehend the patterns in the data. This is where we turn to a technique much used in personality research, namely factor analysis.

Factor analysis is a way of distilling the redundancy that abounds in data such as these. We have already seen that any one of the four variables concerned with travel, competitiveness, social activity, and interest in sex gives you some information about the other three, so it is partly redundant to display all four values for each person. If we just want to see the main trends in the data, we could perhaps calculate a single variable that subsumes these four. If the value for that person on this new composite variable was high, this would be a shorthand way of saying that they are very competitive, very interested in sex, like to travel very much, and spend a lot of time in social activities. A second composite variable might tell you the extent of their vulnerability to depression and anxiety, since these two overlap with each other. Thus, for each person, you would need just two pieces of information, their score on composite variable 1, and their score on composite variable 2, and this would allow you to fill in what is likely to be true of them in the more specific domains. Of course, you would have lost a lot of information about individual idiosyncrasies, since all the correlations are much less than 1, but you would have gained by reducing and simplifying the data.

This, in essence, is what factor analysis does, and I will not go into how it does it, except to say that it is a statistical technique based on the correlation coefficients of all the variables involved, and easily done on any modern computer in less than a second. Let's apply a simple form of factor analysis to the data we have been discussing. The technique extracts two composite variables, called factors. There is no necessity that two factors come out. There could be as many factors as there are variables, if there is in fact no redundancy in the data. However, in this carefully chosen case, two is the number that emerges, and we can display how closely each of the six original variables correlates with the two new composite variables, as shown in Table 2.

You can see what has happened. The technique identifies two underlying patterns. There is something about the people that varies, and that tends to predict a suite of different

Table 2. The factors extracted from six rating scales in 545 British adults.

Original variable	Factor 1	Factor 2
Social activities	<u>0.67</u>	0.01
Travel	<u>0.59</u>	−0.11
Competitiveness	<u>0.50</u>	−0.09
Interest in sex	<u>0.68</u>	0.17
Depression	−0.01	<u>0.85</u>
Anxiety	−0.05	<u>0.85</u>

consequences (social activities, travel, competitiveness, interest in sex). Factor 1 is a kind of statistical placeholder for whatever this attribute turns out to be, which is why the correlations (underlined) between factor 1 and the four original variables are rather large. Then there is a second attribute which is completely unrelated to the first, which says little or nothing about interest in sex or travel, but says a lot about vulnerability to both depression and anxiety (inspect the underlined correlations for factor 2). What factor 1 represents is in fact the personality trait of Extraversion, whilst factor 2 is the trait of Neuroticism. The nature of these traits will be the subject of subsequent chapters. What we have done here is tried to understand the way that traits emerge from data. Personality theorists do not posit their traits *a priori*, or choose them by Cabbalistic speculation, or by any other non-empirical means. In general, they work with lots and lots of data gathered in various ways from real people, and they try to agree on the characteristic factors (as placeholders for traits) that the data reveal.

When ratings for large numbers of behaviours or characteristics are analysed, factor analysis very often extracts exactly five factors. This was noticed as long ago as the early 1930s, and frequently replicated with diverse types of data, but the insight seemed to languish. It was not until the 1980s that a number of different researchers began to converge on the view that there was something special about the number five. Researchers working with a smaller number of dimensions, such as Paul Costa and Robert McCrae, began to realize that they could account for more variation by using a set of five, whilst researchers working with a larger number of dimensions found that they could reliably reduce theirs without too much loss of information. A number of articles began to appear suggesting something of a consensus; namely, you could capture most of the broad-level variation in ratings of behaviour or characteristics of human beings using not less than and not more than five factors. Moreover, the content of these five factors—the big five—is always much the same. They have been given various names and precise characterizations, and we will meet them one by one later, but Table 3 gives a brief overview for those who are not familiar with them.[7]

Table 3. The big five personality dimensions: An overview.

Dimension	High scorers are ...	Low scorers are ...	See chapter
Extraversion	Outgoing, enthusiastic	Aloof, quiet	3
Neuroticism	Prone to stress and worry	Emotionally stable	4
Conscientiousness	Organized, self-directed	Spontaneous, careless	5
Agreeableness	Trusting, empathetic	Uncooperative, hostile	6
Openness	Creative, imaginative, eccentric	Practical, conventional	7

The consensus grows strikingly stronger once we note how well the alternatives to the five-factor model actually fit into it. For example, Raymond Catell is well known for a framework using sixteen personality traits. However, these can clearly be further reduced, since several of them correlate with each other, and when they are factored down, the results are more or less congruent with the big five. Similarly, Hans Eysenck advocated the view that you can capture much of the variation in personality data with just three super-factors, which he called Extraversion, Neuroticism, and Psychoticism. Two of Eysenck's three super-dimensions, Extraversion and Neuroticism, also appear in the big five, whilst his Psychoticism is an amalgam of big five Agreeableness and Conscientiousness. Thus, to get to the big five from Eysenck's apparently opposed position to the big five, you just disaggregate Psychoticism, which was always the most problematic of his dimensions, into two parts, and add Openness. The apparent discrepancies just tend to point the way back to the consensus.[8]

We have then, a consensus on the big five, and a large number of different questionnaires for measuring them, including the Newcastle Personality Assessor at the back of this book. However, all these questionnaires are based on people's self-report of what they are like. It is easy to see how they could be affected by people's mood on the day of taking the test, the way they want to appear, their imperfect self-knowledge, and all kinds of other factors that would render this kind of data unfit to speak of anything but itself. So is there any evidence that scores on these five dimensions are of any use in understanding people's behaviour over the long term?

In fact there is. People's scores are really rather stable over long periods of time. In one study, people took a personality questionnaire on three occasions six years apart. The final scores (twelve years on from the beginning of the study) correlated with the initial ones with r values of 0.68–0.85.

This is extremely high. In fact, it is pretty much the same as the r value you get if people take the test twice with a time interval of six days. It shows that variation due to quirks and accidents of mood is quite limited, and that once you take this into account, the underlying scores are as constant over a decade as they are over a week. People's scores when rating themselves correlate quite well with how others close to them see them, as long as those others know them reasonably well. When strangers rate a target person's personality, there is essentially no consensus between them, but the better they know the target, the greater the consensus. Correlations between ratings from the target themselves and ratings from those who know them well are typically around 0.5.[9]

We can also approach the question of meaningfulness of personality ratings by relating them to direct observations of behaviour, just as Galton urged us to. This has more typically been done in the university laboratory than by gangs of itinerant psychologists jumping out at people all over London, but the results are useful nonetheless. People high in Extraversion really do talk a lot, just as they say they do. When asked to think about or view something stressful or unpleasant, people high in Neuroticism really do become more upset than people low in Neuroticism. When people high in Agreeableness listen to stories, they really do pay more attention to the mental states of the characters than those low in Agreeableness. We could multiply examples here. The more interesting question though, is whether scores on personality inventories really predict outcomes that people outside of academic psychology care about. That is, do they predict outcomes in real life?[10]

There is increasing evidence that they can do, and I will just discuss a couple of examples here. The first is by E. Lowell Kelly and James Conley. Kelly should be lauded for his commitment to this study, as the time elapsed from the collection of the first data point to the publication of the paper was fifty-two years. Data with this level of time depth are a rare and wonderful resource for those of us interested in the long-term patterns of human life. Between 1935 and 1938, Kelly recruited 300 couples, mainly from the US state of Connecticut, who were engaged to be married. Kelly kept in touch with them, collecting data on the state of their marriage—that is, both whether it was intact, and how happy they were within it—in the years immediately after their weddings, again in 1954–5, and again in 1980–1. Back in the 1930s, Kelly had asked five acquaintances of each man and each woman to rate them on personality scales which were forerunners of those we use today. From these, he extracted an average personality score for four dimensions, which were basically Extraversion, Neuroticism, Conscientiousness, and Agreeableness.[11]

The results show the personality scores—those simplistic ratings, filled out by friends back in the thirties—are really rather strong predictors of how the marriages turn out. If either the man or the woman is high in Neuroticism, divorce is much more likely, and if they do stay together, the marriage is less happy, as indicated by the average of his and her independent ratings forty years later. The negative emotions that the high Neuroticism scorer is prone to experience really do make a difference in real life and in the long haul. There are also other interesting patterns. The man's, but not the woman's, Conscientiousness is a predictor of divorce (the lower the Conscientiousness, the higher the likelihood). The accounts of reasons for divorce that Kelly and Conley collected suggest that low Conscientiousness men are basically bad heads of household. Some of them turned out to be drinkers, or others financially irresponsible, or both. Bear in mind that these are couples married before the war, with what we would now regard as a rather traditional gender division of labour. The lack of effect of female Conscientiousness can be attributed to the fact that women of this period did not generally play a provider role.

What distinguishes those who stay in an unhappy marriage from those who divorce is levels of Extraversion and Agreeableness. Again this makes sense. Extraverts are above all very good at meeting people, so it is likely that, in an unhappy marriage, they would tend to find someone else more often than average, and terminate the marriage. As for Agreeableness, my interpretation would be that someone high in empathy and the capacity for fellow-feeling would see when a relationship was causing two people to suffer, and try to work it out one way or another. Someone with less connection to the mental states of others might just go on despite coldness or even hostility.

An even more remarkable study is that begun by Lewis Terman in 1921. Terman was interested primarily in intelligence and its effects on life outcomes. He recruited 1500 Californian boys and girls of exceptional intelligence—a cohort known as the 'Termites'—and followed their development into adulthood. By 1991, half of the male Termites and a third of the female Termites had died. Since personality data had been collected back in childhood, this provided a unique opportunity for Howard Friedman and colleagues to examine the effect of personality on longevity. They doggedly collected death certificates from, as they put it, 'often resistant state bureaucracies', to identify who had died, when, and from what cause.[12]

In 1922, Terman had collected personality ratings of the Termites from teachers and parents. These ratings of course precede the existence of the five-factor model, but dimensions akin to the big five can be extracted *post hoc*. Strikingly, being low on Conscientiousness is a strong predictor of death, increasing its probability in any given year by about 30 per cent. Why would this be? The chief causes of mortality were cancer and heart disease, and those high in Conscientiousness are likely to be protected from these. They smoke and drink less, for a start, and are probably more scrupulous in other aspects of their behaviour too. Friedman and colleagues also found that those who in childhood were optimistic and sociable had a differential probability of dying. The more sociable and optimistic they were, the more likely they were to die. Yes, *more* likely. Though this cuts against an obvious intuition we have about the value of positive emotion, it is explicable by the greater risks that extraverts take, as we shall see in Chapter 3.

These fascinating findings make it untenable to claim that personality ratings are irrelevant, or all in the eye of the beholder, or tell you nothing but some kind of story that the participant is spinning about himself. Being alive and having a successful partnership are profoundly important elements, in both experiential and evolutionary terms, of any human life, and so if some pen-and-paper rating scale that takes ten minutes to complete predicts them, however imperfectly, we should sit up and take notice. We should try to understand how it could be that such a scale could have *any* predictive value given the preposterous and unpredictable complexity of human life. That, of course, is what this book is about.

I said in the Introduction that personality-trait psychology was undergoing something of a renaissance. To need a renaissance, you have to have had dark ages, and personality theory has had those. Through the 1970s and 1980s, there were a lot of problematic results to explain, and widespread scepticism about the value of measuring a few general personality traits. I will spend the rest of this chapter looking at the reasons for this scepticism, and seeing how personality-trait theory has emerged strengthened from its trials.

The first criticism that can easily be levelled at personality-trait theory is that it has a certain circularity to it. Let's consider the following example. When we look at rating data, as we did earlier in this chapter, we conclude that interest in travel, social activities, and sex all go together, and we infer that they are underlain by some common dimension, which we decide to call Extraversion. Extraversion itself cannot be directly observed, or even measured, apart from through its effects on the ratings from which it is inferred. Having identified our dimension of Extraversion, we then use it to explain behaviours and tendencies. If someone talks a lot, we say 'Aha; this is because they are high in Extraversion'. However, 'Extraversion' is *defined* by a load of behaviours which go together, and which include talking a lot. Thus it cannot possibly explain *why* someone talks a lot. We are in the situation of the doctor in Molière's *Le Malade Imaginaire*. When asked to explain why particular concoctions make people sleep, the doctor explains that this is because they possess 'dormitive virtue'. How do we know they possess dormitive virtue? Because they make people sleep of course.[13]

The situation for personality traits is not quite so dire as the circularity of the 'dormitive virtue' example. They do at least tell us which human behaviours tend to co-occur. Nonetheless, it is true that the dimensions of the big five or any personality system as derived from rating data only tell us about the surface covariation of behaviours. They don't automatically provide any explanatory depth. Thus, the criticism of circularity is both true and, as I shall argue, unfair. The criticism is true because if we extracted five factors from rating data and just stopped there, we would have some interesting generalizations about which human tendencies tend to go together, but no real explanations. It is unfair because personality-trait psychologists do not, in general, believe that we should stop there.

Although a great deal of the research effort of the last fifty years has gone into identifying what the major personality dimensions are, this is not, in itself, the end. It is just one step, and an important one at that. We can't get anywhere without identifying the set of important traits, showing which ones are reliably different, and which are reliably the same. This is the stage that most five-factor research has been at, and it is much like doing natural history in Zoology. You find out what is out there, including how many different species you have got. The next stage is investigation of the behavioural foundation of the traits you have identified. In other words, can the traits identified in ratings be related to real-world, objectively observable behaviour and outcomes? The marriage and longevity results discussed above suggest that they can. The stage after that is finding out what the internal basis of the dimensions is. In other words, the ultimate aim is to say *why* some people are more interested in travel than others, or *why* some people are more prone to depression and anxiety. This, of course, is the really interesting stage, and it is this challenge that the current renaissance in personality psychology is beginning to take on.

When we ask a *'why?'* question in the behavioural sciences, we can mean several different things. Sometimes we are really asking about what the structures in the nervous system are whose functioning gives rise to the trait. In the last few years, we have made striking progress on this front, principally because brain-imaging technologies such as PET and fMRI have become available. These techniques allow us to measure the size and shape of particular nuclei non-invasively in the brains of awake individuals, but more than this, they allow us to track the changes in metabolic activity of brain structures as the person responds to a particular task.

Though these techniques are new, they are already yielding evidence that personality traits have a discoverable brain basis. A network of brain areas that have long been thought to be involved in emotions and their regulation differ across people in size and structure, in baseline activity, and in magnitude of activation when particular tasks are performed. These areas include the amygdala, the anterior cingulate cortex, the nucleus accumbens, and parts of the pre-frontal cortex. These differences have been shown by a sizable number of studies to correlate with personality traits as measured by questionnaire (especially Extraversion, Neuroticism, and, to a lesser extent, Conscientiousness), or with other characteristics such as depression that are very strongly linked to personality. Thus, it can no longer be said that the big five personality traits are simply descriptions of behaviour or self-image. It is very likely they will turn out to be shorthand for suites of differences in neural structure and function across multiple brain regions.[14]

Sometimes when we ask 'why?' we mean, how in the individual's development did the pattern arise? This is partly a question of nature and nurture. Behaviour geneticists have techniques for addressing such questions, by comparing the similarity in traits between identical and non-identical twins, or between adoptive and biological siblings. These situations are all experiments of nature. Twin pairs of all types share a common environment, but identical twins share 100 per cent of each other's genetic variation, whereas non-identical twins only share around 50 per cent. For siblings, adoptive siblings share a common environment of rearing, but biological siblings share this *and* also 50 per cent of each other's genetic variation. Thus, by looking at differences in correlations—for example, the degree to which identical twins are more similar to each other than non-identical twins—behaviour geneticists can tease out how much of the variation in personality is accounted for by heredity, and how much by shared environment.

When this is done, studies reliably show that about half of the variation in big five personality traits is associated with genetic variation. Thus, people differentiated by high or low scores on the big five are also differentiated by which variant forms of some of the 30,000 or so genes in the human genome they are carrying. In a few cases, we even have some idea which genes are involved. We will have more to say about genetics, evolution, and the brain in subsequent chapters, but it is clear that in at least two senses of *why*, personality research is moving at speed beyond the merely descriptive stage.[15]

The next issue for personality research that needs some discussion is what has been called the person-situation debate. Broadly speaking, this is the debate about the extent to which someone's behaviour is best thought of as arising from the situation they find themselves in, or from properties of the person himself, or from some kind of interaction of the two. It is often claimed that personality theorists think that only the person, not the situation, is important in predicting behaviour. It is also sometimes claimed that the actual predictive power of personality constructs is dismally low. Neither of these claims is true, but they are so important as to merit examining in some detail.[16]

Critics of personality theory can point to studies that show that the situation people are in is a better immediate predictor of their behaviour than personality scores are. Well, of course. Consider the matter very briefly. Evolution has furnished us with an exquisite set of mental mechanisms that are designed to solve the adaptive problems that our ancestors recurrently faced. Thus, we have fear mechanisms that make us flee danger, attraction and arousal mechanisms that make us choose mates and mate with them, cooperation mechanisms that make us identify and interact with rewarding coalition partners, and so on. The very essence of all these mechanisms is that they are turned on by a particular class of situation (you are in danger), and they facilitate a particular set of responses (increases in heart rate, adrenaline and vigilance, desire to leave, and so on). Devices to map situations to sets of behaviours are what natural selection builds into any organism more complex than a virus. Thus, there is simply no question that a strong predictor of whether someone will be afraid at a given moment or not is whether they are, for example, in a medium-sized cage with a wild bear.

That the situation can have a strong effect on how anxious people feel at any particular moment is thus not really surprising, nor threatening to any sane personality psychologist's world-view. The overwhelming effect of the situation appears especially clearly when we focus on what have been called *strong situations*, as in the bear example above. Strong situations are those very close to the prototype which natural selection designed the behaviour for. A strong situation for fear would be: large carnivore, no cover, nowhere to run, no weapon; whilst a strong situation for sexual arousal might be: maximally attractive available member of target gender, behaving promisingly, in relaxed mood, in intimate setting. Few people would avoid fear in the one case, or attraction in the other.

Life, however, does not mainly consist of strong situations. It usually consists of a bewildering series of much weaker situations. What I mean by weaker is that they contain some cues that might lead them to be categorized a certain way, but are ultimately ambiguous. For example, walking at evening through an unknown neighbourhood, I might perceive some cues potentially indicative of danger; the narrow, shaded streets, large male strangers lumbering about, and so forth. Such a scene may or may not in fact be dangerous. How can one tell? This is where we should expect to see an effect of individual differences. The scene contains enough cues that the anxiety mechanism will get activated if its threshold for activation in a particular person is rather low. However, if the person's threshold is high, he may just enjoy the stroll. Similarly, we all fume if we are directly, gratuitously, and unambiguously insulted, presumably because some reputation-defending mechanism kicks in. However, in an average working week there are probably a dozen interactions that could conceivably be interpreted as subtle slights or insults. Some people don't notice these, some laugh at them, and some become seriously paranoid and enraged. The explanation for the difference is that the threshold for activation of the relevant psychological mechanism differs from person to person.

Thus, there is no conflict between the person and the situation as a source of behaviour in the way I have discussed them so far. Situations trigger mental mechanisms, which facilitate suites of behaviour, but people differ in how easily or how strongly particular mechanisms get triggered by situational cues. In fact, this point has helped us establish a good definition of what personality traits are, namely stable individual differences in the reactivity of mental mechanisms designed to respond to particular classes of situation. It's a rather academic mouthful, but it is a useful working description.[17]

We have not yet dealt with the most substantial issues arising from the 'person-situation' debate. The first of these is that although people's ratings of themselves agree with other people's ratings of them, and are stable over time, this may not translate into much predictive power over behaviour. When rating data from questionnaires are compared to actual behavioural episodes, the correlations tend to be quite weak. This is true as far as it goes, but it is worth remembering that all predictive power in psychology is pretty low. Psychology is not like physics, where you can predict the trajectory of an individual object to many decimal places. The best that any kind of psychology can hope for is *some* predictive power at the statistical level across a group of people. We will never be at the stage of making exact predictions about what individuals will do and when.

Even given this general point, though, it is true that correlations between personality measures and behaviour can be relatively low, particularly when the behavioural measures are based on a one-off, such as what someone will do when faced, on a single occasion, with an experimental set-up. A one-off scenario will be affected by all kinds of circumstantial factors unique to that moment, and so, not surprisingly, you tend to find correlations of 0.3 or lower between behaviour and the person's underlying personality traits. However, once you aggregate to behaviour across multiple instances, the importance of personality becomes much clearer.

Let me illustrate this with an example. For someone who works in a busy office, there could be twenty instances a day of needing something that a colleague is using. For any single one of these instances, being low on the personality trait of Agreeableness might make, say, only a 10 per cent difference to the probability of snapping irritably at that colleague. For predicting snapping in any single episode, then, the power of the personality variable is quite weak. However, aggregated across all instances, low Agreeableness will mean an average of one extra bout of irritable behaviour per day, or five per week, or more than two hundred per year. This is a hugely important difference that is bound to have an impact on a person's life, and yet it stems from what, in the single shot, is only a very slightly raised probability of annoyance. The more we aggregate behaviours across multiple instances, the more important personality as a predictor becomes.

The cumulative effect of small differences in behaviour becomes even more marked when we consider that the traffic between the person's behaviour and the situation can flow both ways. To return to our busy office, my snapping irritably at colleagues might make them so annoyed that they deliberately dawdle when using something I need. They might find subtle ways of antagonizing me to teach me a lesson. In particular, other people in the office who are low in Agreeableness will have a particular reaction to my reaction. Instead of ignoring it or laughing it off, they will spoil for a fight, and actually seek out chances to get into confrontations with me. Thus, I will experience a different set of situations because of my personality disposition, and the indirect effect of my low Agreeableness will be that I have many more fights.

Such effects of personality on situations are very common. Why do extraverts have more casual sex than anyone else? It may be that many introverts would also like to do so, and if given the appropriate situation, they would. However, they don't seem to find themselves in that context. Extraverts are more likely to talk to strangers, get to know people more easily, and go to more parties, parties that are of course full of other extraverts. Indeed, a party is essentially a device for allowing extraverts to find each other (if you have one, they will come!) Thus, extraverts make a set of choices that lead to situations where the contexts that lead to casual sex are readily available. Even if the act itself is entirely determined by situational cues, extraverts will have it more often simply because of their choice of situations. This kind of relationship between personality and situation is called situation selection.[18]

Situation selection can be contrasted with situation evocation. This is where, as in the Agreeableness and office arguments example, we elicit a reaction from others that perpetuates or exaggerates a tendency that we already have. Another example would be transitions into and out of marriage. You might think that marriage and divorce were quintessential examples of externally originating life events. Thus, we would count them as powerful situational determinants of behaviour. However, both the tendency to get into marriages and, as we have already seen, the tendency to encounter disharmony when in them, are powerfully influenced by personality. There is actually a substantial genetic effect on both the likelihood of marriage and the likelihood of divorce, as evidenced by the relatively similar marital histories of identical twins. The thoughts and feelings we habitually experience evoke in the other either the desire to marry us or the wish that they weren't married to us, so when we count marital status as a 'situational' variable, we may be overlooking the subtle effects of the person.[19]

The power of situation selection and situation evocation is probably rather great, and it has become clear in the last couple of decades that if behaviour often follows from life events, life events often follow from personality. Indeed, the propensities to experience positive and negative life events have recently been found to have substantial genetic heritability, since identical twins are much more similar in terms of life events than fraternal twins are. The only explanation for such a finding is that there is inherited variation in personality, and this leads, through situation selection and situation evocation, to similar patterns of situations. Indeed, life itself can be seen as a meandering run through possibility space, in which each act we perform has an effect on the landscape of eventualities we will face next. By mature adulthood, at least in affluent and liberal societies, life consists in responding appropriately to situations that we have in significant part, consciously or unconsciously, chosen for ourselves.[20]

Because of this effect, and because of the power of aggregation, studies that monitor people's behaviours in real time—using something like a diary or a pager—always find the following patterns. Individuals' behaviours vary strongly from moment to moment and from context to context. Even introverts sometimes can't stop talking, and even people very high in Agreeableness have the occasional argument. However, for the introvert, not being able to stop talking is a much rarer event than it is for the extravert. They are just not so often in contexts that push them over their threshold for this behaviour to happen. Thus you find very reliable differences in the frequency of feelings and acts that are related to the big five. In consequence of this, a person's behaviour averaged over a reasonable period—say a couple of weeks—turns out to be a very strong predictor of their behaviour in the next couple of weeks. We each have a characteristic way of being, and aggregating our behaviour across a range of contexts allows that way of being to emerge. This way of being is very important, since each one of the major personality dimensions has been shown to have consequences for life outcomes, as we shall see in the coming chapters.[21]

There are also important questions concerning the appropriate breadth of personality traits. People's behaviour is often self-consistent over time, but the consistency is highest when the situation is exactly the same. For example, in a classic study of moral behaviours in children, cheating on a test by copying answers predicted cheating on a subsequent similar test by copying answers rather well, but predicted cheating in a different type of test by adding points to one's score somewhat less well. Thus, we would predict behaviour better with a narrow construct like 'propensity to cheat in tests with a key where the answers can be copied' than with a more general trait such as 'honesty'.

Because of this, some psychologists have argued that personality traits should always be defined relative to a class of situation rather than just stated unconditionally. In one sense, all personality traits already do this. Neuroticism, for example, is the overactivity of negative emotions, and therefore to say that someone is high in Neuroticism must mean saying that they will react strongly when in that class of situations that can be appraised as containing a threat to the self. However, this leaves unanswered the question of how broad or narrow the classes of situation should be. Should we measure Neuroticism in general, or, say Neuroticism about disease, Neuroticism about colleague approval, and Neuroticism about personal relationships separately? When you use the narrower sub-traits, you get higher self-consistency than when you use the broad one. However, you still get some self-consistency—a substantial amount, actually—when you use the broad one, and of course you get it across a much broader range of situations. Even in the children's moral behaviour study, the correlations between the different types of cheating were well above zero.

So what do we need to measure, a few broad traits, or lots of narrow sub-traits? The answer is that we can do both. Measuring the sub-traits will give us maximal predictive power for a rather limited set of situations. However, there is also (somewhat weaker) self-consistency across very broad suites of situations, and it is this self-consistency that broad traits such as the big five capture. It is because of the weak self-consistency of Neuroticism that we can predict that in general people who worry about disease will also worry more than average about other things.

Why do these very broad traits exist? Why would the amount you worry about disease be a significant predictor of the amount you worry about social relationships? After all, you might have had a history of dependable and reliable relationships, but some unsettling brushes with disease. The answer must be that the mental mechanisms that underlie worrying about disease share brain circuitry with the mental mechanisms that underlie worrying about other things. Any variation in the responsiveness of those shared circuits will show up in all kinds of worrying, not just one kind. It's a bit like a car. The handbrake and the footbrake do different jobs and have some separate components, but they also rely on the same hydraulic system. As a consequence, a loss of brake-fluid pressure will show up in reduced effectiveness in both brakes. The more two components draw on shared machinery, the greater the extent to which the performance of one will be a predictor of the performance of the other.

Each of the big five, then, should be thought of as variation in some underlying brain circuit which affects a whole family of related psychological functions. Each of those psychological functions will also be affected by non-shared circuits, which is why the intercorrelations are not perfect. We have seen that a suite of things such as interest in sex, interest in travel, interest in social activities, and competitiveness, all go loosely together to form the Extraversion family. What links these diverse behaviours? I shall argue later that they all draw on the same brain reward circuits. We know that the same brain structures are involved in the anticipation of rewards as diverse as seeing an attractive opposite-face, receiving money, receiving food, and taking an addictive drug. It looks like natural selection has built up our complex psychology of different types of reward—adventure, sex, attraction, sociality, and so forth—by running more and more feeds from some much more primitive original mechanism, whose deep ancestral function was, say, move towards things which look like enhancing your fitness. If that shared mechanism is a bit more active than average in your brain, you will tend to be more drawn than average to many classes of rewarding activities, not just a specific one.[22]

Different psychological mechanisms can share resources because they have a shared evolutionary history, because the design brief they perform is structurally similar, or because they are often needed together. Some combination of all of these can also be true. Either way, it is costly, difficult, or unnecessary for natural selection to make related mechanisms totally functionally independent in a brain that must have been built up piecemeal from a simpler ancestor. Thus it is no surprise that there are families of psychological mechanisms drawing on shared or overlapping resources.[23] Whether researchers study a narrow sub-trait or a broad one depends on what their purposes are. Narrow sub-traits maximize your predictive power for some very specific behaviour. On the other hand, the broad big five give us a much more synoptic view of the ways individuals vary, including the interesting question of how all the different quirks that individuals have cohere together and stem from a smaller number of underlying characteristics. Since a synoptic view of personality is the objective of this book, I will concentrate almost entirely on the broad trait level from now on.

We have established some key points in this chapter. Personality traits are meaningful, stable, partly genetically inherited consistencies in classes of behaviour. They can be measured using ratings. They come to have predictive power when aggregated over many instances, and as well as affecting our responses to life events, they affect which life events we are going to have. The many narrow traits that make up any one person's temperament tend to cluster, so that five broad trait families—the big five—emerge and can be usefully studied. In Chapters 3 to 7, we will meet each of the big five in turn. First, though, we must turn to the question of evolution. Where does the variation in the big five come from, and why has natural selection allowed it to persist?

2

The Beak of the Finch

If for each environment there is a best organism, for each organism there is a best environment.

Lee Cronbach

The finches of the Galápagos Islands are justifiably famous for inspiring Darwin's theorizing about evolution. There are some nineteen sizable islands and dozens of smaller islets in the Galápagos archipelago. Each one has a slightly different flora, and therefore each presents a slightly different challenge for a small bird in search of dinner. What Darwin noticed in his time on the Galápagos was that the finches on different islands had slightly different beaks. Where there were large seeds to be cracked, beaks were thick and powerful. Where there were holes to be explored, beaks were thin and slender. Darwin's explanation was that although the finches had all descended from a common ancestor, those closest to the optimal beak size for the island they were on had had a greater than average chance of surviving and reproducing. Since big-beaked parents have big-beaked offspring, and slender-beaked parents have slender-beaked offspring, the populations on each island had gradually come to diverge in their beak characteristics. This of course is natural selection in action, and natural selection produces variation in organisms across varying habitats.

There is, however, a second interesting aspect of Galápagos finches that is relevant to our current theme. There is also variation *within* each island's finch population. If you plot the frequency distribution of beak sizes on an island, there is a clear central tendency, but there is a wide spread of beak sizes either side of this average. Beak size is highly heritable, which means that it is largely transmitted genetically. This raises the question: if there is an optimal beak size for each island, why doesn't every finch on that island have it? Why, in other words, would there be genetic variation for beak size *within* an island's population as well as *between* islands?[1]

This question is identical to one we need to ask about personality, namely, why is the variation between individuals there? Because this question is so important for everything that follows, we will, in this chapter, be making a short excursus into evolutionary biology. Personality traits in humans are heritable, just as beak size in finches is. Heritable means related to differences in genes. The genome is made up of many different genes (around 30,000 in the human case). Each of these genes, when activated, has some biological effect, such as causing the synthesis of a particular protein that is used in our cells. Very often, a gene exists in two or more variant forms in the population. Such variants arise because of genetic mutation. That is, in the copying of genes as sperm and eggs are made, and cells divide, errors may on rare occasions creep in, such that the new genetic sequence differs from its ancestor by some repeated, deleted, transposed, or altered sequence of genetic code. Once a mutation has happened, the individual bearing it will have a chance of passing it on to their children, who may pass it on to theirs, and so a mutation that starts out in one individual has the potential to become widespread in the population if circumstances and chance aid its spread.

Some mutations make no difference to the gene's functioning, but some change the structure of the proteins that are synthesized, and that of course affects how our cells actually work, to a greater or lesser extent. In the most dramatic cases, having a genetic variant causes some massive dysfunction, as in cystic fibrosis or Apert's Syndrome. More commonly, the genetic variant will cause a much more subtle effect, such as making you reject most blood transfusions, or producing a particular protein very slightly more or less efficiently. Variation in the genome is relatively abundant. Surveys of human genes suggest that more than half of them have a variant that actually makes a difference to how it does its job, and that exists at some appreciable frequency in the human population. Very often, there will be an overwhelmingly common form, and a rare variant, and we may simply interpret the latter as a mutated version that has arisen recently and hung around locally for a while, but will go extinct fairly quickly. In other cases, though, the rarer forms are not so rare, and show every sign of being ancient in origin, since they are widely dispersed across humankind.[2]

We can now rephrase our 'why?' question about variation within a population. Let's focus for the moment on beak size. Certain genetic variants will make the birds carrying them have a thicker beak (they make keratin a bit more efficiently, or they continue growing for longer, or something). On the islands where the optimal beak size is thick, the birds carrying those variants will be the ones who survive and reproduce best. The ones carrying the alternative, thin-beak variants will leave fewer offspring, so that, over the generations, they tend to reduce in proportion until they disappear. In other words, on islands where thick beaks are best, we might expect that the population would come to consist only of those with 'thick-beak' genetic variants. There should be no genetic variation left within the population of a single island.

Another way of saying this is that mutation creates genetic variation, and then natural selection winnows it. Winnowing is the agricultural practice of losing all the waste matter in order to be left with just the best stuff. And this is what natural selection does; the genetic variants that make individuals that are best suited to the local environment gradually increase their frequency in the population, until nothing else is left. This winnowing effect has also been called 'Fisher's fundamental theorem'.[3] Natural selection reduces genetic variation.

To return to personality, we might imagine that there was an optimal threshold to have for how easily one's negative emotions were evoked. Natural selection would have wiggled about a bit to find this optimum, but once it had found it, it would spread like wildfire, and we would all have the genetic variants that produced exactly this level of threshold. However, the fact that twin and family studies show that Neuroticism is heritable shows that this is not in fact the case. Significant heritability means that there are different genetic variants affecting the negative emotion threshold out there in the population, and we will tend to get the ones our parents had. Why then, has Fisher's fundamental theorem not proven true in this case?

It has become something of an article of faith amongst evolutionary psychologists that, because of Fisher's fundamental theorem, genetic variation in characteristics important to survival and reproduction will be rather rare. Thus, Leda Cosmides and John Tooby suggest that genetic variation in humans is restricted to 'functionally superficial' traits like blood group or eye colour, whilst all important psychological mechanisms will be 'species-typical', by which they mean the same in all normal individuals. This is obviously not true. In humans, there is strong evidence for heritability in intelligence, personality characteristics, height, and many other attributes. It is beyond question that these all affect survival and reproduction. One just has to point to the examples of personality in relation to marriage and longevity that we have already met in this book. What then could be going on?[4]

Tooby and Cosmides actually make several related points. The first is that we should not expect the human or any other population to contain individuals with qualitatively different sets of mental mechanisms. This is because mechanisms are built by suites of dozens of genes all working together to produce the complex final design. Let's say you had just one negative emotion system, which you used to avoid all kinds of threats in your environment, whereas I had two, one designed to detect threats from people, and the other, using a completely separate brain region, designed for threats from the inanimate environment. Each of these is quite a reasonable design, and there is no strong *a priori* reason to think one would be better than the other. Now let's consider a population that contains some of the one-type, and some of the two-type individuals. Every time we make a baby, we shuffle the pack of mum's and dad's genetic material.

The unfortunate children in this population might end up with about half the genetic material they needed to make two separate brain threat-systems, and also about half the material they needed to make a single unified one. If you have half the ingredients to make a great soufflé, and half the ingredients to make a chicken curry, you end up with something that is not a good soufflé *or* a good curry. You end up with a mess. This would be even more true when you ended up with just half of each of the integrated suites of genes you needed to make an emotional circuit that worked. Fifty per cent of an integrated suite of genes is not as good as 100 per cent. It is probably not even 50 per cent as good. It is probably completely useless. Sexual reproduction, then, selects strongly for a species-typical basic architecture. When you mate with someone, you are relying on them turning out to have the same basic kinds of blueprints as you, so that when your two genomes are sampled into the baby's genome, the resulting mixture is a functional whole, not a non-soufflé non-curry.

The demand for reproductive compatibility, then, means that we shouldn't expect a single population to contain *typologically* distinct individuals.[5] This is one reason why personality schemes which divide people into discrete 'types' are biologically implausible. But what of the variation we do find? If you look at the examples I have discussed—height, personality, intelligence—it is clear that these are basically *continuous* dimensions. There is genetic variation in height, because there are lots of ways genetic variants can cause the growing programme to go just a bit faster, or go on just a bit longer, without disrupting the overall coordination of the system. Most of the significant genetic variation there is, then, consists of variants making an incremental difference to the development or functioning of some system that we all share. Everyone has a body with the same basic body plan, but its size varies from person to person. Everyone has the same negative emotions, but in people high in Neuroticism they are relatively easy to evoke. Everyone has the same cognitive apparatus, but in some people it works a bit quicker or more efficiently than in others. This is always worth remembering in research on individual differences; we are just dealing with continuous variation over a set of universal mechanisms.

We still haven't dealt with why variation would persist along these continuous dimensions. Tooby and Cosmides assume that usually there will be an optimal place to be on the continuum in terms of reproductive success, and that the winnowing action of natural selection will go to work until everyone has the genotype most likely to produce this optimal value. They concede that there could be 'some thin films' of continuous genetic variation on some characteristics, but don't seem to think they will be very significant. My only quibble with their position is that I think the films might not be so few, so thin, or so very insignificant. To tackle the question of why films of continuous variation in important characteristics can persist despite the winnow of selection, let us return to the Galápagos. Fortunately, thanks to the Herculean efforts of biologists Peter and Rosemary Grant, a great deal is known about how these finch populations change over time and about how the environment affects their evolution.

In 1977, on the small islet of Daphne Major, there was a severe drought. The size of the population of Darwin's finches crashed from around 1400 to around 200 individuals, as most died of undernourishment. The small seeds on which the birds normally fed became rare, and the only possible avenue to survival was to eat larger, tougher seeds that the birds would normally ignore. The Grants measured the thickness of beaks in the population both before and after the drought. Before the drought, the average beak size was 9.5 millimetres, with a spread of observed variation around this mean. The survivors of the drought were drawn disproportionately from the larger-beaked end of the distribution, so that in the post-drought population, the average beak size was now about 10.5 millimetres. This is natural selection at work, using ecological conditions to pull the population towards a new, larger-beaked form.

This is all very well, but why does it lead to the maintenance of variation? If drought conditions went on year after year, you would soon have a population all of whom had beaks of 11 millimetres plus. But the fact is that drought conditions don't occur year after year. In fact, in 1984, the weather was unusually rainy, and small, soft seeds abounded. In this year, it was the birds with relatively small beaks who were most likely to survive and reproduce, so the population was tugged back in the other direction. Thick beaks have the benefit of allowing one to tackle large thick-coated seeds, but clearly have some cost, probably making it more difficult to handle the small soft seeds efficiently. The optimal balance of these benefits and costs clearly varies with the precise local conditions. If you are a finch born in 1977 with a sleek and slender bill, you are, unfortunately, eight years ahead of your time. If you are born in 1984, son of a line of highly successful thick-beaked bruisers, you are going to find yourself out-paced by a bunch of slim kids with sports bills. As Coriolanus said in a rather different context, ripeness is all.

The winnow of selection, then, fluctuates. Even on one very small island, its pull is quite inconsistent along the con-tinuum of beak size. In any given year, there is a best beak size to have, but it is not the same best from year to year. Given this inconsistency, it is very hard for selection to make the population converge on a single beak-size genotype. Just as it is working hard for a few years to eliminate all the small-beaked guys, the wind changes direction and now it finds it is increasing the small-beaked ones and decreasing the thick-beaks. This oscillation goes on, ceaselessly, but because of its changeability, selection can never settle on one, universal optimum. Even if there is one beak size that over many years is the best on average, then episodes of fluctuation in selection make it much more difficult for selection to settle on just that optimum and eliminate all other variation.

One way heritable variation can persist, then, is through *fluctuating selection*. For fluctuating selection to retain variation, several conditions must be met. First, being high or low on the continuum must have both benefits and costs. If having a thick bill makes you do best when there are droughts and also best when the year is wet, then there is no game on. Thick bills will simply prevail. Only if thick bills are good in some contexts and bad in others will variation persist. Second, there must be fluctuations in the relationship of the trait to survival and reproductive success. In our example, the fluctuations were from year to year, but similar effects can operate in space, too; at the top of the island, the optimum size might be slightly different from at the bottom, due to the pattern of vegetation. The fluctuations can even be due to what others in the local population are doing. For example, it could be that if everyone else has huge beaks and is cleaning up all the big seeds, then you could do quite well as a small-beak eating the scraps they ignore, even if big seeds are the most common type available. Or, if they are all feasting with their small bills on the abundant soft seeds, you might still do better as a large-bill by avoiding competition with them and finding yourself some tough nuts to crack. This kind of effect is called *negative frequency dependent selection*. It simply means that sometimes you will do well just as long as your type of individual is rare in the population. As your type becomes the most common one, individuals of some other type might then start to do well because there are few competitors for their niche. Negative frequency dependent selection is a powerful way of maintaining genetic variation in a population, but it is really just a sub-type of the more general phenomenon of fluctuating selection, the fluctuations in this case being due to the composition of the local population.[6]

The final condition is that a reasonably large number of genes have to contribute to variation in the trait. If the number of genes involved is very small, then genetic variants will be lost from the population by chance or between fluctuations, and it will be a long time before they are replaced with new mutations. Several genes being involved ensures a steady supply of new variation to keep the process going.

Fluctuating selection is not the only force that can lead to the maintenance of genetic variation. To investigate the major alternative, let us consider the train of the peacock. We all know about how peacocks use their splendid, fan-like train to catch the attention of dowdy, but, to the peacock, fanciable peahens. As it turns out, the peacocks with the most elaborate trains are the most fancied by peahens, with the result that they father the overwhelming majority of peachicks in wild populations. No monogamy here, remember; the males with the most elaborate trains can impregnate many females, leaving many more misshapen males with no offspring at all.

Despite this, there is considerable heritable variation in train elaboration. This is puzzling. The selective advantage of males with the genes for elaborate trains is so overwhelming you would imagine that within a few generations only their genotype would be left. The genes for simpler trains would have gone extinct, and rapidly at that, leaving a single train genotype that led to maximal elaboration. To understand why this does not happen, we need to consider the numbers of genes involved.

Growing an elaborate train is hard. They are big and extremely expensive in terms of energy and protein. You can only grow a perfect one if all the machinery of growth metabolism in your body is working perfectly. If you get infected by chronic disease, it will divert energy from the train-training business and you won't be able to do it, so your immune system needs to be working well in order to grow a perfect train. If you can't absorb energy from your food, you won't have enough for train feathers, and so your gut needs to be working well to grow a perfect tail. If you are rubbish at finding food and avoiding predators, you won't have enough energy spare, so your brain needs to be working well to grow a perfect train. In short, growing a perfect train requires so many resources that it is hardly an exaggeration to say that everything about you needs to be working well in order to do it. Now if every system in your body needs to be working well in order to grow it, then a genetic mutation that has a negative effect on any system in your body is going to show up, indirectly, in your train. Your train is a kind of curriculum vitae of how well you are doing, and for this reason, it is known by biologists as a *fitness indicator trait*.

When mutations arise in genes, their most common effect is to make the system work a bit less well. It is easy to see why. Take your car, and randomly mutate one of the components, like the spark plug or a light bulb. Make it a little bit bigger or smaller, or change the relative sizes of its subparts. You might make it work better, and if you did, your new design could get adopted throughout the car industry. More likely, though, it won't work so well. This is because the component already has a great deal of design history built into it, and you are just tweaking it at random. There are lots of ways of working badly, and only a few ways of working better than it does already, and your random mutation is overwhelmingly likely to find one of the former. Mutation, then, usually makes things work less well.

Given that there are many genes in the genome, and that each one has a small chance of mutating with every generation, there are quite a lot of mutations around. It has been estimated that each of us carries one or two new ones that arose in the production of sperm and egg by our parents. In addition, we probably each carry about 500–2,000 mutations that arose earlier in our family history, and whose destiny is to be winnowed from the population in the fullness of time. The load of mutations will in general be rather unequally distributed, and when we mate with someone, we want to choose an individual with as few as possible, because we want to give our little ones an unmutated start in life. This is why the peahen looks at the peacock's tail. He is saying, 'look at me; imagine how few harmful mutations I must be carrying in order to have built *that*'. And indeed, Marion Petrie has shown that the offspring of peacocks with elaborate trains don't just have elaborate trains themselves; they are also better at surviving. The males with the best trains are simply of higher genetic quality overall, and they pass this to their offspring of both sexes.[7]

Variation in fitness-indicator traits such as the peacock's tail persists *despite* extremely strong selection acting to winnow it out, and it persists because of the sheer number of genes involved. With thousands of genes able to affect the display of the trait, and with each of these having a chance of mutating in every generation, then variation just comes faster than even the strongest selection can winnow it out. Everyone has some harmful mutations. The contest simply becomes who has fewer than his competitors.

Fitness-indicator traits, then, retain population genetic variation through the force of mutation alone. This is a different type of situation from that of fluctuating selection. In fluctuating selection, having more of the trait is sometimes good for you and sometimes bad, dependent on local conditions. For fitness indicators having more is always better. It is just that it is difficult to get more because of the weight of mutation. For fluctuating selection, a reasonable number of genes need to be involved, perhaps a few dozen, in order to keep injecting variation. For fitness indicators, thousands of genes, potentially the whole genome, need to be able to affect the trait in question. For fluctuating selection, the offspring of an individual high in the trait will be better than its competitors under some conditions, and worse than its competitors under others. For example, if you are a female finch, mating with a thick-beaked male is a smart move if there is a drought coming up, and a bad one if there is a wet year around the corner. By contrast, the offspring of an individual high in a fitness-indicator trait will always do well relative to its competitors. If you are a peahen, you should always mate with the male with the most elaborate train, regardless of the long-term weather forecast.

In this book, I will argue that personality variation in humans is maintained by the fluctuating selection type of mechanism rather than the fitness-indicator one. This is an argument from plausibility rather than a well-demonstrated fact. Personality seems to me to fit the fluctuating selection model for a number of reasons. It is really quite easy to

identify situations in which a higher level of any given personality trait would be useful, but also situations where a
higher level would be harmful. It looks like there are both
costs and benefits to moving along the personality dimensions, not just benefits. In fact, at the extremes, personality dimensions always become pathological, and this is very
different from the situation with respect to peacock train
elaboration, where more is simply better, and less simply
worse. Moreover, many of the heritable traits in other species
which look most like personality differences are demonstra-
bly maintained by fluctuating selection, as we shall see in the
rest of this chapter. However, I could turn out to be wrong,
and variation in one or more of the big five might turn out
to be maintained in some other way. Only time and further
research will tell.

This is not to say that there are no examples of fitness-
indicator traits in humans. Physical symmetry is one obvious
one. More symmetrical men are perceived as more attractive, and have more sexual partners, than the rest of us.
There is no drawback to being more symmetrical; you do
it if you can. Geoffrey Miller has made what seems to me
to be a convincing case that intelligence is another example
of a fitness-indicator trait. Contrary to popular belief, intelligence doesn't just measure 'book smarts'. Intelligence tests
correlate with reaction time and spatial abilities, and predict
performance at practical jobs and tasks that have little to do

with academic or scholastic learning. Whatever they measure is some kind of index of how well the nervous system is
running overall. Intelligence is also positively correlated with
physical symmetry. There is really no known disadvantage,
other things being equal, to being more intelligent. In so far
as variation in intelligence is genetic (and, importantly, this is
only partly true), being more intelligent probably just means
'having relatively few mutations that impair the operation of
my nervous system'. The idea that intelligence is a fitness-
indicator trait is thus a plausible one. I just think personality
traits have a quite different character, as we shall see.[8]

The beak of the finch is a morphological trait. That is, it is
a variation in the structure of the body. Is there any evidence
for genetic variation in behavioural traits in animals? In fact,
there is plenty. All kinds of continuous traits that have been
studied, in many different types of organism, tend to show
variation. In particular, biologists have identified personality
traits rather akin to those we see in humans in many different
species. Dimensions analogous to all of the big five have been
spotted in chimpanzees, whilst even the spineless octopus
has dimensions rather like Extraversion and Neuroticism. Of
course, identifying a personality dimension in a non-human
species is a different business from human research. You have
to print the questionnaires on water-proof paper for a start.
Seriously, in the animal case we rely on observer rather than
self-ratings of individuals' behaviour, but otherwise many of

the techniques are similar. Just as in the human case, behaviour should ideally be self-consistent over time, should be reliably identifiable by different observers or using different measurements, and should affect actual outcomes in some ecologically appropriate context. Sometimes it has been possible to show that animal personality traits are heritable, just as they are for humans.[9]

The best animal studies have a power rarely seen in studies of humans, because, animal life cycles being so much faster than ours, researchers can follow the fortunes of different personality characteristics over several generations. Where they have done so, they provide powerful support for a fluctuating selection account, and so for the rest of this chapter, I examine two examples in detail.

The first comes from that charming and mischievous little fish, the guppy. It turns out that individual guppies vary in terms of how they behave in the presence of a predator, their natural predators being larger piscivorous fish such as the splendidly named pumpkinseed. When put in a tank with a clear partition through to an adjoining tank containing a pumpkinseed, some guppies will swim closer than others to the predator, and stay near to it for more of the time. This tendency is rather consistent within individuals on repeated trials. Some guppies are simply disposed to be more wary than others. In a classic study, Lee Dugatkin assigned guppies to three groups; high wariness, medium wariness, and low wariness, using an adjoining tank task of the type I have just described. Then he did the bit that you can't do with human subjects. He put guppies from each group into a tank with a pumpkinseed.[10]

After 36 hours, 14 out of 20 high wariness guppies were left alive, compared to 7 out of 20 from the medium-wariness group, and 5 out of 20 from the low-wariness group. After 60 hours, there were no low-wariness guppies left alive at all, whereas 8 of the 20 high-wariness had survived. In short, Dugatkin had shown conclusively that the presence of a predator strongly selects for wariness. Surely, then, there should only be wary guppies out there by now, as their non-wary siblings were yesterday's breakfast. How does variation persist?

The answer comes from a related study of guppies from several different populations all over Trinidad. Some guppies live upstream where waterways are too narrow to house piscivorous intruders, whilst others live downstream where these predators can lurk. Shyril O'Steen and her colleagues showed that if you take guppies from different habitats and place them in an artificial pool with a predator, then those from upstream locations with no predators are more likely to get eaten than those from downstream. You might think that this could stem from their learned experience with predators, but no. When guppies are caught and bred in tanks, then the offspring whose parents come from downstream habitats survive better in a predator pool than those whose parents were from upstream, even if they have no experience of predators themselves and it is a type of predator that their parents would never have seen.[11]

The best explanation, then, is that there is heritable variation in wariness in the presence of predators. In a downstream environment, selection pushes the population towards high wariness, but upstream, there is no such push. In fact, there seems to be selection *against* wariness, since when a new population is set up in a predator-free habitat from a source that lived with predators, the level of wariness goes down over a few generations. Whenever you are looking out for predators, you are not feeding, resting, or mating, so if there are no predators and you are spending time looking out for them, your fitness is going to suffer relative to your more laid-back competitors. Only when predators turn up will you have the edge.

This naturally raises the question of why there aren't two different species of guppy, a wary one that lives at the bottom of streams, and one that has no anti-predator behaviours that lives at the top of streams. One reason is that upstream and downstream habitats are not isolated from each other. Guppies migrate from one to the other, especially downstream, so there is constant remixing of the two types. Moreover, the presence of predators is not an all or none situation, and the distribution of predatory fish will vary over time.

When streams are running full they may venture further upstream. Thus selection is constantly changing over time and space, as the benefits and costs of vigilance tussle with each other. The result is that if you consider the population of guppies as a whole, what you see is a broad distribution of heritable differences in wariness. No specific level of wariness is globally favoured by selection, though for every individual guppy there is a level of wariness that it would be best to have.

Our second example comes from that familiar garden bird, the great tit. Personality and its effects have been studied in exquisite detail in this species in a series of recent studies by Niels Dingemanse and his colleagues in the Netherlands. Dingemanse and colleagues first established that there were individual differences in exploratory behaviour in the birds. They showed this by capturing them from the wild, giving them what amounted to a personality test, then releasing them. The test consisted of allowing the bird to enter a laboratory room with five artificial trees in it. The researchers then measured the number of flights or hops around that the bird made within the first two minutes in the room. 'Fast' explorers made many hops or flights, and covered more of the space than 'slow' explorers, who tended to be rooted to the spot. Now since the birds had been ringed, the researchers could identify when they had caught the same individuals again. Individual birds turned out to be somewhat self-consistent over time in their pace of exploration.

Even more interestingly, the researchers could tell from the rings which birds were parents and offspring, and which ones were siblings. This allowed them to estimate the genetic heritability of the exploration trait. Their estimate is that about 30–50 per cent of the variation in exploration style was heritable. This is the same kind of range as found for human personality traits.[12]

Just as we ask whether human personality traits have any consequences in real life, so we want to ask whether exploration style has any consequences outside the laboratory for a great tit. It turns out that it does. Dingemanse and his colleagues looked at seven years of data on the natural behaviour of great tits at their field sites, comparing various life outcomes to the scores that birds had marked up on the exploration task when they had been captured. Parents who were 'fast' explorers had offspring that travelled further from the natal nest in their fledgling year, and ended up breeding further away than their 'slow' explorer counterparts. In addition, the researchers were able to establish that birds born outside the study site who had ended up breeding within it had 'fast' exploration scores. Thus, fast explorers clearly venture further and wider than slow explorers.

What effect does exploration have on reproductive success? The answer, pleasingly to me, is that it depends. The researchers looked at the relationship of personality to survival and reproduction in three years in particular: 1999,

2000, and 2001. It turns out that 2000 was a good year for great tits, because the beech trees of the Netherlands seeded heavily. They do not always do this, and indeed did not do so in 1999 and 2001. In the tough years of 1999 and 2001, winter food availability was low. However, every cloud has a silver lining, since this meant that there were not so many surviving great tits around when the days began to lengthen, and so competition for spring territories was less intense than usual. In the good year of 2000, by contrast, winter food was relatively abundant, so there was less competition for it, but many more birds made it through the winter, so there was strong competition for territories in the spring.

In 1999 and 2001, females who were 'fast' explorers were significantly more likely to survive, plausibly because their greater activity and aggression gave them an edge in competing for scarce winter food. In 2000, though, 'fast' females were actually less likely to survive. Their overt aggressiveness and excessive activity may have been unhelpful when there was plenty for everyone. The males tell a different but complementary story. The survival of males is critically influenced by their ability to compete for and hold territories in the spring. In the good year of 2000, with so many competitors around, territory holding was a bird-eat-bird business, and those with the 'fast' exploration style did best. In the poor years of 1999 and 2001, competition for spring territories was relaxed, and the 'fast' exploring males actually did

worse than the 'slow' ones, again because they probably bore
the costs of unnecessary aggression.

The right type of exploration score to have, then, depends
critically on accidents of your birth. If you are a male born
into a good year, then a 'fast' style is going to help you in
spring competition, but if it is a poor year, this will not be so.
If you are a female born into a bad year, then a 'fast' style will
help you compete for scarce resources, but if it is a good year,
it will be a hindrance. Given these constant localized fluctuations, natural selection can never fix one single genotype in
the population.

I chose the guppy and great tit examples because the
personality dimensions that they present are so tantalizingly
similar to human Neuroticism and Extraversion, respectively.
They are not the only possible examples, but they are well-
studied ones which furnish us with a lot of useful principles.
In each case, there is a heritable behavioural dimension with
a suite of effects that are good for reproductive success under
some circumstances, and bad under others. In each case, it
is possible to work out just what those costs and benefits
are, and the circumstances under which they come into their
own. Are we able to work out the costs and benefits for the
human personality traits too? With this in mind, we now turn
back to the big five, beginning with the irrepressible trait of
Extraversion.

3

Wanderers

Erica, at 55, is living a quiet life. Her pretty cottage in the downland of southern England stands in a little wooded valley, where, she tells me, deer and rabbits are her neighbours. At around 8am, she drives her little hatchback ten miles up the road to an office in another out-of-town location, which she shares with a couple of other journalists who work with her on her small magazine. She gets on well with her colleagues, but after work, her day is quiet; she drives back, with no rush-hour traffic to worry about, makes dinner, watches some television, and goes early to her bed, where she has, as she puts it 'vivid, entertaining, cinematic and revealing dreams'.[1]

Erica might not seem a promising person to tell us about the nature of Extraversion. Extraverts are supposed to be ambitious, go-getting and, in the broadest sense, lusty, whereas Erica writes of her life goals: 'I just don't seem to have any. I don't especially want a promotion (though like anyone else, I would like more money). I don't aspire to fall in love'. She describes an idyllic but largely solitary and unambitious existence. Nonetheless, Erica scored very highly on a five-factor Extraversion scale when she took it a couple of years ago. I was intrigued to look more deeply into her story to find clues of how and where in her life her Extraversion surfaced.

The first clue is that she has a simple explanation for her lack of ambitions. 'I have achieved virtually all of my youthful dreams', she writes. And how. She had always wanted to write professionally, and she does. She had wanted to learn a foreign language and to live abroad, and she had lived in Italy for over a decade. She had, like many people, dreamed of being a pop singer, but unlike most, she actually attained her dream. In Italy she had sung with a band and had a real following. So, the quiet life is not looking quite as quiet as all that. Before arthritis set in, she says, she was 'a tireless walker, horseback rider, sailor, bicyclist, yoga practitioner and dancer'.

Erica was then, a person of great drives and desires, and there is evidence that this also found expression in her romantic life. She writes candidly:

I also spent my entire life, from puberty onwards, utterly driven and ruled by my high sexual appetite. Until I met my husband, I was compulsively promiscuous. Being with him took care of that; we had a wonderful sexual relationship for some years, but as he aged, his sexual drive slowed. . . . When we moved to Italy, I began having lovers, married Italian men; there were two with whom I remained close for many years . . .

What unites the disparate elements of this rich life story? The desire to travel, the sexual desire, the tireless and varied activities, the musical performance? To answer this question, we need to delve a little further into the nature of the Extraversion trait.

The terms Extraversion and Introversion were introduced by Jung as long ago as 1921. He wanted to describe two alternative orientations towards the world. Jung's extravert is focused outwards; he loves action more than reflection, and other people's company more than his own thoughts, and is consequently outgoing and active. Jung's introvert, by contrast, is oriented to his own thoughts and feelings, and consequently is seen as somewhat aloof, and wants solitude and peace to reflect. The concept of Extraversion has shifted over the years (and despite the shared names, Jung's psychological types don't entirely map onto personality traits of the sort described in this book, for various reasons). However, all theories of personality, not just the five-factor model, contain a dimension which is very similar to Extraversion as I describe it here, and which has Jung somewhere in its intellectual ancestry.[2]

In popular consciousness, and in some earlier psychological theories, the central part of Extraversion was sociability. It is certainly true that high Extraversion scorers spend more time in social activity than low scorers, are more talkative, like parties more, and like to be the centre of attention. They are quicker to form new social relationships, as shown for example in a study of students going off to college; the more extraverted ones were quicker to strike up new friendships than the more introverted ones.[3]

However, we should be careful in equating Extraversion with sociability. First, shyness is most often due not to low Extraversion, but to high Neuroticism and anxiety. The low Extraversion scorer is not necessarily shy. He simply doesn't get that much out of social activity and so can often do without it. For this reason, low scorers are often seen as aloof. We should also not confuse high Extraversion with good social relationships. Extraversion is a predictor of how much a person will like going to parties, how much time will be spent in social activities, and the facility in striking up new friendships, but it is not a predictor of how well those friendships will go. In the study of college students, harmoniousness of relationships with other students was predicted by another trait, Agreeableness, and not by Extraversion at all. Indeed, extraverts can be quite socially difficult if they are not also high in Agreeableness. They are the kind of people who get a kick out of going to a party, getting drunk, and ending up in a stand-up row with someone they have never met before. Extraverts low in Agreeableness have no compunction in cutting someone dead in front of others, and may even relish doing so if they get something out it. (I am not suggesting Erica is like this, since her Agreeableness score is high.)

We need, then, to understand the nature of the extravert's interest in social interaction, and perhaps this is best done by seeing what else comes under the umbrella, for Extraversion has several other facets. Extraverts enjoy sex and romance. They tend to be ambitious (though of course the content of their ambitions will be highly idiosyncratic), and enjoy gaining status and receiving social attention. They are prepared to work very hard in pursuit of fame or money, though they also enjoy their leisure pursuits. They like active sports, travel, and novelty. All in all, they are perceived as highly active people who can lay their hands on vast stores of energy in pursuit of goals. There has been debate over the years about how much of what we might call impulsivity belongs under Extraversion. By impulsivity, I mean behaviours like taking an unplanned personal or financial risk, betting or drugs, flirting with the law, or needing a bit of danger in life. These kinds of behaviours are in the shared territory of Extraversion and another dimension, Conscientiousness, though for most of the damaging ones, such as addictions, Conscientiousness turns out to be the better predictor. There is in fact a clear conceptual distinction between the two dimensions, which will become apparent in due course.

There is one final constellation of tendencies which belongs to Extraversion and which is, in fact, the key to all the others. Extraverts have a lot of positive emotion. In their daily lives, high Extraversion scorers consistently report more states of joy, desire, enthusiasm, and excitement than low scorers. You can see this in what they write. Erica, for example, even when talking about what is now a relatively uneventful existence, tells me that she is 'delighted' with her routine. She 'love[s] the lacy patterns that moonlight casts on her butter-yellow walls'. Her work situation is 'a gem' with 'wonderful' colleagues. She says that though staying home doing chores and chatting on the phone doesn't sound too thrilling, 'I seem to love it', and lower-case letters are simply insufficient to describe her response to her Saturday mornings: 'I LOVE to stay in bed, reading, drinking coffee, taking a nap'. Her whole account is thoroughly perfused with descriptions of states of positive emotion. Even taking part in my study was a 'fabulous opportunity', and she ends by hoping 'that I have successfully conveyed to you my predominant mood, which I believe is optimistic and humorous'.[4]

What are the positive emotions? They are all activated in response to the pursuit or capture of some resource that is valued. Desire is awakened in us to get us to go and look or work for the thing we want. Excitement builds towards the anticipated capture of that resource. Joy follows its capture. These are all states to do with getting things, or moving towards getting them. But which things? Common recurrent foci of positive emotions are attention from potentially important others (making new friends), status (getting a promotion or writing a best-seller), material resources (a pay rise), gaining a new mate, mastering a new skill or challenge, or simply being in a pleasing location. All of these events which elicit and organize positive emotions can be referred to as *incentives*.

There are two kinds of incentives in the world. Unconditioned incentives are those things which people (and animals) find just naturally rewarding. You don't need to teach rats to eat when hungry or to prefer sucrose solution to water. You don't need to teach kids that having a friend is nice, or heterosexual adolescents that the opposite sex is strangely exciting. Unconditioned incentives give us a warm and energizing feeling, and this pairing of feeling with outcome is not learned. It has been set up innately, by evolution, presumably because, over many generations, those individuals who got excited at the thought of eating when hungry were more likely to survive, and those who got excited at the thought of mating were more likely to reproduce, than their rivals. Analogous evolutionary arguments can easily be made for all other unconditioned stimuli, be it gaining status, gaining a coalition partner, or mastering a skill.

Then there are conditioned incentives. Recall Pavlov's famous dogs, who salivated in response to the production of food. A bell was paired with feeding time, and eventually, the dogs would salivate to the bell alone, because they had learned that it predicted food. A bell, which is naturally a meaningless stimulus, had come to have incentive value through conditioning. Human incentives are very often conditioned, in quite complex cultural ways. Money, for example, is something that most people find to be a strong incentive, but this cannot be an unconditioned relationship. Rather, people have acquired a conditioned pairing of gains in money with some natural incentive. You might think that this natural incentive would be the intrinsic pleasure of consuming goods and services, but, at least in the affluent West, this does not seem to be entirely the case. Various lines of evidence suggest that our interest in money—and the material goods it buys—is mainly as a marker of comparative social status. People with lots of money and lots of visible goods to prove it are perceived as higher up a status hierarchy than people who live in other ways. Social status appears to be the unconditioned incentive that anchors both the Protestant work ethic and the excesses of consumerism.[5]

Positive emotion mechanisms in the brain, then, detect cues of either unconditioned or conditioned incentives available in the environment, and organize our behaviour towards capturing them. They make us wake up, take interest, and do what we need to do to capture the reward, be it filling in the application form or chatting her up. There is nothing unique to humans about such mechanisms. When an amoeba follows a chemical gradient to reach and then ingest some food, we might say that it is acting on its positive emotions. All sensate organisms have some kind of system for finding good things in the environment and going after them, and the suite of human positive emotions is just a highly developed system of this kind.[6]

Let me flesh out the argument that it is the strongly reactive positive emotions that make sense of all the diverse behaviours associated with Extraversion. We have already seen that Erica has had plenty of positive emotion in her life. So too has Bill, another of my correspondents with a very high Extraversion score. Bill, who is in his fifties, comes from a blue-collar Midwest family of Scandinavian origin. A very successful entrepreneur, he was worth several million dollars by the time he was 40. He tells me:

I had all the insignias of money and power: a farm, horses, a Porsche, a forest, and a penthouse in the nearby city.

Bill, in his own words, 'got careless and lost everything in less than a year'. His marriage also ended, about which he appears philosophical. He currently lives in a hotel in Colorado, which gives him room and board in return for working as a ski instructor (like so many extraverts, Bill has a physically active vocation). One might imagine that Bill's rise and fall from the world of material success would make him stoical about its appeal, but not a bit of it. He says:

I have one aim and that is to get rich again. I know that I can do it, and I know how good life is as a rich man. Life is only worth living when you are rich ... I do not want to retire. I want to work until I die. I am learning Russian because I consider Russian women the prettiest and most ambitious ... I want to marry a girl from the Ukraine and show her the good life.

One cannot but be impressed by Bill's optimism, determination, and derring-do, considering he has dragged himself up to millionaire standard once, lost everything, and is clearly quite prepared to do the whole thing again. More than anything, it is evident that he wants to do all these things not because he actually needs to, but because he gets a tremendously powerful buzz out of taking on challenges and capturing the rewards. In a wonderful statement of the male extravert credo, he says:

There is nothing better than to win a struggle. I love taking risks. I love standing in front of people and talking, telling them how

beautiful life can be... My greatest success was a speech I gave
for 250 people at a business congress and to hear them applauding
afterwards. It still rings in my ears.

Just as Erica's strong response to incentives sent her to Italy,
into rock music, and into the arms of her Mediterranean
lovers, Bill's strong response to incentives drove him to work
hard, drive a Porsche, court beautiful women, and get up in
front of crowds at a business congress. All of these things are
rewarding, naturally or by conditioned association, and so
any normal person would get a lift from them. But perhaps
not quite as strong a kick as Bill gets.

Let us imagine for a moment that Bill's positive emotion
systems were a little *less* responsive. If the kick he got from
the prospect of owning a Porsche or indeed a forest(!) were
a little smaller, he would probably not be prepared to put
in quite so many hours to get it. If Erica got a smaller kick
from romance, she might have avoided the risks and costs of
complex extra-marital entanglements. It can't have been easy
to become a minor Italian pop star. I dare say the hours were
awful, the knocking on doors humiliating, and it probably
cost her more money than she made, at least early on. So it
really wouldn't be worth doing unless the buzz was very big.

If Bill and Erica's positive emotions are very strongly
responsive, what would the life of a person whose positive
emotions were less responsive be like? Obviously, they would

experience less positive emotion. Note that this is not the same thing as saying that their life would be full of negative emotion. The opposite of joy and excitement is not fear and sadness. The opposite of joy and excitement is simply the absence of joy and excitement—emotional flatness, if you will. Numerous studies have shown that the amount of positive emotion we have in our lives is no predictor of how much negative emotion we have. Some people are troubled neither by much joy nor many tears, whilst some have precipitous highs *and* crashing lows. Thus, a person relatively unresponsive to incentives is not necessarily a sad person. Instead, they will be a little more aloof when it comes to the fleshpots of this world; they will, like anyone, be drawn from time to time to sex, and parties, and status, but the kick they get will be relatively small, so they are not going to break a leg to get there. As any economist will tell you, if the return from an activity is made smaller and the cost remains the same, you are going to consume less of it than you did when the return was bigger. So someone with a relatively small response to incentives would be less inclined to slave those extra hours for a little more money or fame, drive all the way across town to be at that party, or upset a perfectly satisfactory marriage for some erotic experimentation.[7]

This more measured approach to incentives is evident in some of my less extraverted correspondents. Andrew is 25 with a good degree in computer programming. He currently lives with his parents, and has some good friends who he often sees every week. At times, though, he won't see them for a few months, and this is clearly not a huge problem. He has been to Scotland a couple of times (about a day's drive from where he lives), but that's about it as far as travel goes. As he puts it, 'I kind of like exploring places and kind of don't'.

Andrew's computer programming skills are (I would have thought) highly marketable in today's economy, and he is clearly a talented young man, as he makes and manipulates electronic music on his computer. However, he doesn't seem to want to go out of his way to get rich and famous from either his music or his computer programming. He will sooner or later land a substantial job, but he is not naïvely excited about this prospect. He tells me:

I don't really have a lot to look forward to. I mean, as soon as I find a stable job, I can move out and live wherever, get a girlfriend, buy a ton of stuff I don't need, maybe get married, create children, buy them stuff... then maybe die or something like that.

I think there is great, stoical depth to these comments. They also tell us a great deal about the motivation of the introvert. One might hastily categorize Andrew as a bit miserable and depressed, which I don't believe to be correct. It is true that one aspect of depression is *anhedonia*, which is defined as a lack of pleasure in normally pleasurable things. There is a definite link between anhedonia and low Extraversion. However, in depression, anhedonia is bundled up with a mass of fears and anxieties. I see none of these in Andrew. He is not in the grip of negative emotion. He just clearly understands that the kind of stuff that people sweat to get—material possessions, marriages, careers, and so on—are fine, but don't have *that* much of an effect on him. So he will take them if they come, and if they don't, I don't think he will be too bothered. He could make a perfectly satisfactory life either way, just as he will see his friends if they are around, but not fuss if they are not. The introvert is, in a way, aloof from the rewards of the world, which gives him tremendous strength and independence from them.

The contrast to Bill, who simply must become rich again, and longs to have applause ringing in his ears and a Ukranian beauty by his side, could not be more clear. Another introvert who contrasts nicely with Bill is a research scientist from Bethesda, Maryland, called David. David was doing cutting-edge biochemical research, but his institute failed to secure funding, so he was gradually pushed into teaching and maintenance work. He now gets little chance to do original research, and expects to lose his job quite soon. Imagine the blow that this would be for someone like Bill. Now look at David's reaction:

I expect to become unemployed in the near future. I see this as an opportunity, since it would give me freedom and would relieve me from participating in the rat race of performing uninteresting tasks in exchange for money and status, both of which I am not interested in.

Clearly, these big incentive-laden goals don't do enough for David to make him want to go out and fight for them. Instead, he is quite happy observing, contemplating, learning, and developing his garden.

We can, then, identify the heart of what Extraversion is all about. Extraversion is variation in the responsiveness of positive emotions. In the high scorer, the responsiveness is great, and so the person is prepared to work hard to get the buzz of company, excitement, achievement, adulation, and romance. The low scorer's positive emotion systems are less responsive, so the psychological benefits of getting these things are fewer. Given that the costs of getting them are the same for introvert and extravert alike, the introvert is not so motivated to do so.

There is quite a lot of scientific evidence that this account of Extraversion is correct. In one study, participants wrote for a few minutes about either a horrible or a nice experience that they had had. They reported their present mood both before and after the writing. Extraversion scores predicted how much better their mood would be after writing about the nice experience. In a follow-up study, participants watched film clips that were either amusing, fearful, sad, or disgusting. Extraversion scores predicted how much better the participant's mood would be after the amusing clip. High scorers got a big mood lift, whilst low scorers got a more modest one. Extraversion scores did not predict the size of the emotional reaction to the negative clips, and so Extraversion cannot be about emotional reactivity in general. It is about emotional reactivity to just the class of rewarding or pleasant stimuli.[8]

Brain imaging has begun to confirm this view. In one recent study, participants viewed pictures with either negative emotional associations (such as crying people, spiders, guns, or cemeteries) or positive ones (a happy couple, puppies, ice creams) whilst in a Magnetic Resonance Imaging machine. The MRI scanner, in its functional version, allows the metabolic activity of different parts of the brain to be measured with considerable spatial and temporal resolution, by tracking the signal from oxygenated blood. The study found several brain areas where the size of the increase in metabolic activity when the image was a positive one was positively correlated with Extraversion score. That is, high scorers got big increases in these areas when they saw a puppy, and lower scorers got smaller increases. There were different brain areas where metabolic activity increased in response to negative images, but the size of this increase was predicted by another personality trait, Neuroticism, and never by Extraversion.[9]

Research on non-human animals has also helped elucidate the brain mechanisms underlying positive emotions. Deep inside the mammalian brain is a network of structures, including those called the ventral tegmental area and the nucleus accumbens, where neurons increase their rate of firing in response to cues of imminent reward, such as a squirt of sugar solution. This is shown by implanting a tiny measuring probe into the brain, and obviously this can't be done in humans. However, we can now look at the activation of the areas non-invasively, using functional Magnetic Resonance Imaging (fMRI). Just as in the rat experiments, there is an increase of activity in immediate anticipation of a squirt of a very sweet beverage called Kool-Aid onto the tongue of the participant. Those people with a particularly large increase in activity turn out to be those who are risk-takers on a computer game played for points. Moreover, the increase in activity in this and connected brain areas is found in response to many other types of reward, such as money or attractive opposite-sex faces, not just sugar.[10]

We have known for around fifty years that if a tiny electrode is implanted in one of these regions in a rat's brain and hooked up to a lever, the rat will press the lever all the time, even to the exclusion of eating and drinking, in

order to deliver stimulation. The mid-brain reward structures project forward into a number of key structures in and
underneath the cortex of the brain, so they have a powerful
capacity to influence decisions. They contain a population
of neurons which use the neurotransmitter dopamine, and
because of this association, dopamine has become known as
the brain's reward chemical. Though this is almost certainly
simplistic, there are clear relationships between dopamine
and incentive motivation. Drugs with a stimulating effect
on dopamine neurons, such as cocaine, cause feelings of
pleasure and euphoria and are powerfully addictive, whilst
increasing mid-brain dopamine activity in rats increases sexual, exploratory, and food-capture behaviours, which can
all be thought of as approaches to rewards. In humans,
the physiological response to a drug that has dopamine-like
effects in the mid-brain is linearly related to Extraversion
scores.[11]

There is converging evidence, then, that what makes an
extravert an extravert is a high degree of responsiveness in
a suite of dopamine-driven brain areas including the ventral
tegmental, the nucleus accumbens, and their projections,
whose function is to fire us up when there are cues of
reward in the environment. The low Extraversion scorer has
a smaller response in this system, and so goes less out of their
way to follow up such cues. But how would some people
come to get a larger response in these areas than others?

We know that around half the variation in Extraversion score appears to be genetic, so there must be some genes which play a role in building this system and whose variants are responsible for its varying levels of responsiveness. Knowing that dopamine circuits were implicated in incentive-driven behaviour, researchers genetically engineered mice with much increased effective levels of dopamine activity. The mice were hyperstimulated, running about in a frenzy of excitement even in a rather dull empty cage. Mice genetically engineered to lack the ability to make their own dopamine are just the opposite: they won't even approach food or drink when hungry, unless, that is, they are injected with artificial shots of the precursor of dopamine.[12]

The next step was to see if there were naturally occurring alternative forms of genes which are involved in building the dopamine system in humans. If there was a variant that moved people just a little way towards the 'hot' rats, or just a little way towards the lethargic ones, it might explain some of the population variation in Extraversion. Two studies published in 1996 seemed to show exactly this. There is a gene called D4DR which codes for a receptor molecule to which dopamine binds and which allows it to pass signals between neurons. As it turns out, D4DR varies substantially between individuals. There is one sequence of forty-eight pairs of DNA bases on the gene which repeats itself, but the number of repeats is not always the same. Some versions of the gene have as few as two repeats of the sequence, whilst others have as many as eleven. The most common forms are four repeats and seven repeats. Each of us carries two copies of D4DR, and since one comes from mum and one from dad, they need not be the same version.

Both studies showed that people with one or more copies of a 'long' form of the gene (that is, one with at least six repeats) had higher scores on a personality trait related to Extraversion. Their methods and their sample populations were, encouragingly, quite different, so it seemed as if the phenomenon must be real and general in its application. However, though a substantial number of studies have since found the association, others have failed to do so. The consensus at the moment is that there is *some* kind of relationship between variation in DRD4 and traits related to Extraversion. For example, it has just been reported that the variants of the gene people carry are what predict the strength of their sexual desire. However, the DRD4 length repeat alone has a very small effect on personality, which is why not all studies have been able to find it, and moreover, there are complex interactions between several different parts of the gene and with other genes. These tend to obscure any linear mapping between the number of DRD4 repeats and personality traits. None of this should surprise or disappoint us unduly. We should expect a trait like Extraversion to be affected by variation in a relatively large number of genes, which interact in a complex way. The point is that variation is clearly heritable, and dopaminergic incentive systems are clearly involved.[13]

The long form of the DRD4 repeat seems, from its distribution today, to have arisen many thousands of years ago, and looks like it has increased in frequency in the manner of a genetic variant that confers a selective advantage. However, if the advantages of the long form were completely unalloyed, it would have increased much more consistently, and we would all have two long forms by now. Instead, it is likely that bearers of a long form sometimes have advantages and sometimes disadvantages.[14]

This leads us to the broader question of how evolution shapes the distribution of Extraversion. We have seen many reasons why high Extraversion scorers do well. They can, like Bill, take on enormous challenges with gusto, and sometimes succeed, gaining themselves status and resources. There is a more or less linear relationship between lifetime numbers of sexual partners and Extraversion. Like Erica, high scorers tend to have casual matings and affairs, as well as more marriages than low scorers. In the ancestral environment, this may well have meant higher lifetime reproductive success, especially for men, who benefit more in fitness terms from additional partners. Thus, we can see plenty of reasons why high scorers might often have done well over recent evolutionary history.[15]

In Chapter 2, though, we saw how, for great tits, being a fast explorer was a good thing in some ecological contexts, and very definitely a bad thing in others. Could something similar occur with human Extraversion? In general terms, if you are off chasing some new reward, you are not looking after what you have already. Remember how Bill lost his millions much faster than he made them. He is not completely forthcoming on how this happened, but I suspect that he was in pursuit of some even greater goal, and in the excitement of this, did not husband his wealth prudently. A more cautious man could have lived comfortably for the rest of his life on what he had, though a more cautious man probably would not have made it all in the first place.

Then consider Erica. Her husband had to be very tolerant of her transgressions. As it happens, they had no children, but if they had, there is a real risk they would have ended up not living with their father, given the colourful marital history. Since high Extraversion scorers have an increased likelihood of affairs and of multiple marriages, their children are disproportionately likely to end up living with step-parents. Exposure to step-parenting is the strongest known predictor of child abuse, and exposure to divorce has measurable detrimental effects on children's outcomes. The rich but unsettled life of the extravert can thus entail real risks.[16]

These risks can also be much more direct. Extraverts are always zooming about, doing physically active and risky things. A study of bus drivers found that those who have accidents have higher Extraversion scores. In a study of mine, adults who had been hospitalized as a result of accident or injury had higher scores than those who had not. In the study of the life histories of the 'Termites', optimism in youth, which we may consider a proxy for Extraversion, predicts an earlier death. The researchers attribute part of this to more drinking and smoking, and the rest to some unidentified lifestyle factor, which I would bet is rushing around pursuing thrilling rewards.[17]

The costs and benefits of Extraversion are, then, finely balanced. Amongst our ancestors, it seems to me that some extraverts in some contexts probably did very well, but that others were reckless and ended stickily. Introverts have always been more dependable. The optimal level of the trait in terms of fitness would have thus fluctuated with the details of the local context, including what everyone else was doing. Geneticist Yuan-Chun Ding and his colleagues have suggested that where the local environment was depleted or rapidly changing, selection might favour individuals with a restless tendency to explore and pursue potential rewards, whereas where resources were abundant and the environment stable, this would be an unnecessary and hazardous

temperament to have, and more cautious individuals might
do better.

This intriguing theory can be related to the recent history
of humankind. One hundred and fifty thousand years ago,
our ancestors were restricted to parts of tropical Africa. By
the time of the agricultural revolution less than ten thousand
years ago, we were found on every continent. Ding suggests that this expansion would be led by restless, wanderer
types, responding to resource depletion at home by seeking
new possibilities further away. Intriguingly, the prevalence
of DRD4 long forms is higher in nomadic societies than
sedentary ones, and very high in populations such as native
South Americans who have made long migrations within the
last several thousands of years. Such a pattern is suggestive
of an advantage to the DRD4 long forms precisely when it is
advantageous to be a wanderer.[18]

Most of the variation in traits like Extraversion, though,
is within-population rather than between populations. The
optimal level of Extraversion would usually have depended
on the social niches and opportunities within the very immediate context of the surrounding few dozen people or few
miles. The ceaseless oscillation in costs and benefits of
incentive-driven behaviour would have meant that we never
settled on a single, uniform, incentive-related genotype.

This oscillation brings us back to a central theme of this
book. There is no right or wrong level of Extraversion, no

level which is intrinsically good or bad. I don't believe Erica's life is any more or less worthwhile than Andrew's. Having a certain level is simply part of the background against which you have to make your life choices, a topic we will return to in a later chapter. Seductive though it might be, there is no more point in me wishing myself to have a higher or lower level of Extraversion than I have than there is for me to wish I were, say, born in 1777, or in Papua New Guinea. I have to make some sense of being born in England in 1970 with the Extraversion score I have. However, just as it is worthwhile to understand the age in which one lives, it is worthwhile understanding the nature of Extraversion, not least because at some point in life you will have extended interactions with someone whose level is different from your own. If you marry someone with a higher score than you, they will sometimes want to do things which seem pointless, costly, and difficult to understand, be it going out partying, buying a Porsche, or taking up some crazy new hobby. If on the other hand you marry someone with a lower score than you, you will occasionally feel disappointed that they just don't want to do as much as you do, and they fail to get really enthusiastic about your latest scheme. Don't worry. It's just how they are wired up.

4

Worriers

Some people seem to get all the bad luck. Susan seems to have hit on a seam of bad men. As her high-school years in a London suburb drew to a close, she was pondering what to do with her life next. The teachers thought she was good enough—the brightest they had ever taught, in fact—to try the competitive entrance examination for Oxford University. However, not only would she not do this, but she would not even put in an application for a second-tier, or any other, university instead. She had a notion she would apply to Art School, but after making a fact-finding visit, she found the rate of attrition from the course too worrying. So what would she do next?

As she puts it:

My solution came along very soon. A group of my friends had started going to a local youth club and asked me along. Within a couple of weeks I met the first love of my life, destined to be my first husband. Adam was a house builder, he made quite a lot of money and he seemed glamorous and a lovely boy. We were in love and wanted to get married and so I left school and got a job in an office . . . I lost touch with my friends who went off to university whilst I played house.

The idyll did not last, however. She says 'the job started to bore me and I began to wonder if I was doing the right thing with my life. We got married within a couple of years, and I began to feel unwell soon afterwards'. The unwellness that Susan is talking about was clinical depression. She lost weight rapidly, had trouble coping, and started to miss periods of work. She was given a series of different antidepressants. This was barely 1980, and antidepressants had more side-effects than they do now. The doctors kept changing the prescription in the search for one that was effective without being too disabling.

As for her marriage, Susan writes 'Much as I wanted to be the perfect wife, something was very wrong but I still don't know what it was'. The warning signs were there. Adam had a bad temper, and had hit her on a few occasions before they were married. In time, he became controlling and abusive. He would make sure bills came from her salary, and tell her what to wear and do, whilst being free himself to go out drinking with friends. The violence increased as the depression deepened.

This was a period of black isolation for Susan. It came to an end, finally, when she met, and developed a 'crush' on, a local jazz musician. The crush became an affair. During this time, Adam was increasingly cruel and suspicious. Under the weight of her ill-health, she gave up her job. Adam was not happy about this. 'He had no intention of keeping me . . . He wanted me to keep on paying the household bills so that he had disposable income to command for whatever he wanted. Violent and severe beatings were becoming more regular during this time and he knocked me out a couple of times, and broke my nose on more than one occasion.'

She plucked up courage to leave and moved back in with her parents. It transpired that Adam too had been having an affair anyway. Susan enrolled for college, to study nursing, and began life again without a care in the world. Well, not quite. Her new partner, the musician, turned out to be married, and a notorious womanizer. Though they stayed together for five years, he never really made any commitment to her, often two- or even three-timing her. 'He treated me appallingly, looking back', she says.

Some years later, Susan finally extracted herself from her relationship with the musician and met her second husband, Steven. Steven, she writes, 'was a bit of a sad case (always drunk and penniless) and I felt sorry for him'. She didn't think the relationship would go anywhere, but 'to most of our colleagues' amazement' they got married a couple of years later. Things seemed good at first, but it became clear that Steven was not doing well at work, and had some unexplained changes of job. 'Steve was increasingly later and later back from work, and obviously the worse for drink when he did get back. He also seemed reluctant to hand money over and there were mysterious delays with his pay'.

Steven's drinking got worse and worse—though he would deny it—and culminated in job loss, and, eventually, some nasty bouts of aggression towards his wife. When he finally beat up their daughter, the police were called, and Steven is under an injunction not to come near. Through this upsetting period, Susan had several more episodes of depression, taking the newer medications that were by now available. By now she was working for a large retail chain, where she came under the remit of a bullying manager, whose behaviour drove her to suicidal thoughts. After more time off work, she was granted a severance deal from her employer that will tide her over for a little while.

Susan's life is an eventful and moving story, in which there is more to be investigated. I have chosen it to illustrate the trait of Neuroticism, on which Susan's score was very high. I have chosen it for the wealth of detail and honesty she brings to it, and because it illustrates not just some of the obvious features of Neuroticism, but also some of the more subtle ones. Before we go back and examine the details, though, let us consider what scientists know about Neuroticism.

Neuroticism is to negative emotions what Extraversion is to positive ones. Recall the experiments where high

Extraversion scorers show a big increase in good mood when they watch a funny film clip, or write about a great experience. When people are asked to watch a frightening or upsetting film, or write about a bad experience, it is their Neuroticism scores that predict how big the negative turn in their mood will be. We also know that high scorers are more affected by the hassles of daily life than low scorers. Neuroticism seems, then, to measure the responsiveness of negative emotion systems.[1]

What are the negative emotions? An interconnected group including fear, anxiety, shame, guilt, disgust, and sadness, they are all deeply unpleasant to experience, their unpleasantness presumably being a design feature to teach us to avoid experiencing them. If positive emotions are designed to make us locate and go towards things which are good for us, negative emotions are designed to make us detect and avoid things that would, in the ancestral environment, have been bad for us. Thus, fear makes us vigilant to potential dangers, and makes us wary of the feared thing. Anxiety makes us search the environment and our minds for possible problems and hazards. Disgust keeps us away from that which is noxious or infectious. Shame and guilt are complex emotions, but seem at root to deter us from acts with negative consequences. Finally, there is sadness. Sadness is a strange emotion, and its function is not fully understood. Some have argued that it is a social signal, that says to important others,

'I am not coping here, give me support'. There is another school of thought that argues it is a kind of energy-saving withdrawal from a plan that has failed, and then again those who suggest a cognitive function. During the dark, honest rumination of sadness, we re-evaluate failed goals and past mistakes, and make better plans for the future. All of these possibilities may be true. What is clear is that sadness is a negative emotion that shares a lot of psychological machinery with other, more high-arousal feelings such as anxiety.[2]

It is worth dwelling a little on the design features of the negative emotions. They operate according to what has been called 'the smoke detector principle'. Smoke-detectors are designed to alert you to the presence of fires. Given this, they can go wrong in two ways. They can either go off when there is in fact no fire (a 'false positive') or fail to go off when there is in fact a fire (a 'false negative'). The former is mildly annoying, but the second is catastrophic. Therefore, when adjusting the sensitivity of a smoke alarm, it makes sense to set it at such a threshold that it will *always* go off when there is a fire, even if that sensitivity comes at the cost of periodic false alarms. Next time you are stuck outside a building as a consequence of a groundless fire alert, console yourself that a well-engineered smoke detector is set at the level required to produce essentially no false negatives, and thus will give you a pointless wait in the rain from time to time. If you engineered one that was less sensitive and never produced false alarms, it would miss the occasional real fire, and someone might die.

Very similar reasoning applies to the negative emotions. They were all originally designed to detect serious hazards, such as risk of death from predators, loss of social position, or the risk of social ostracism. All of these would have been death sentences for most of our ancestors. Given the costs of missing real threats, it made sense for natural selection to engineer them to be hypersensitive in various ways. Far better a little groundless worry than getting eaten or starving. This is all very necessary as far as nature-red-in-tooth-and-claw is concerned, but its unfortunate corollary is the following: even when your negative emotions are working correctly, most of the worries you have will be completely groundless. If you lie awake at night worrying about a possible offence you caused an influential colleague, you are probably doing so needlessly. You are doing it because you come from a long line of people who lay awake at night worrying, and thus never got into trouble. Their rivals who did not lie awake at night worrying were happier than your ancestors, but from time to time they made some catastrophic errors of judgement and got attacked, eaten, or expelled.[3]

Spare a thought, then, for high Neuroticism scorers. Within the population, there is clearly a bell shape of variation in just how smoke-detector-like those negative emotions are, and high-Neuroticism scorers are in the tail of the curve. This means that, if the modal human being is worrying groundlessly 80 per cent of the time that they worry, then the poor old high-Neuroticism scorer is probably worrying needlessly 99 per cent of the time that they worry. Moreover, there are so many things out there that are marked with at least some sparse cues of potential worrisomeness that your high scorer is going to be worrying a great deal of the time.

The specific ways that negative emotions are hypersensitive are first, that they go off in response to things that have even a small probability of being indicators of real threats, and second, that once even partly roused, they cause a hypervigilance to threat in perception, attention, and cognition. An anxious person is quick to detect an angry face, and has trouble disengaging attention from it when it is there. An anxious or sad person will make the negative interpretation of ambiguous words such as dye (die) or pane (pain). Similarly, negative emotions make people respond to the news of bad events in the most catastrophic way possible ('It was all my fault', 'Everybody hates me', 'I will never succeed', versus 'I did my best but circumstances were against me', 'Those people are misguided', 'It will go better next time').[4]

What your ancestors needed to survive is not what you need to have a pleasant life, and this is especially true for high Neuroticism scorers. Evolutionary reasoning also gives us useful insights into why the disorders of negative emotion have the forms that they do. We fear rejection, stigma, illness, open spaces, strangers, and the unspoken negative intentions of others, precisely because these were all contexts of real danger for our ancestors. All such phobias and disorders of mood and anxiety are strongly predicted by Neuroticism scores, as we shall see.

In the case of Extraversion, it was possible to make some putative links between emotional systems, brain regions, neurotransmitters, and genes. This is also possible for Neuroticism. Just as there are some brain regions the magnitude of whose response to positive images such as ice cream and puppies is related to Extraversion, there are regions the magnitude of whose response to negative images such as guns, angry faces, and cemeteries is related to Neuroticism. Central to this circuit is the amygdala, a nucleus lying under the temporal lobe on each side of the brain. As well as being more responsive to negative stimuli, the amygdala is more active at baseline in high-Neuroticism scorers. Moreover, there is some evidence that amygdala size or density differences are actually associated with Neuroticism or depression.[5]

Associated with the amygdala is the hippocampus, and an area of the right frontal lobe called the right dorsolateral prefrontal cortex. This region shows reduced activity and volume in depressed patients, and, in healthy volunteers, it becomes very active when they are trying to suppress a negative feeling. We will find out more about this brain region in the next chapter, but it is plausibly involved in using knowledge to damp down automatic negative emotional reactions. Its underactivation in depression reflects the failure of control of negative emotion in this condition.

At the hormonal and neurochemical levels, several substances are involved in negative emotions. The hormone adrenaline, for example, is integral to anxiety, which is why preventing its action using beta blockers can be effective for panic attacks. Patterns of secretion of the stress hormone cortisol become dysregulated in long-term negative emotion conditions. The substance that has attracted most interest, though, is the brain neurotransmitter serotonin. Serotonin appears integral to the functioning of the regulatory circuit for negative emotions. I will not dwell on the evidence for this here, but it includes brain imaging of specific molecules, the effectiveness of serotonin-targeting drugs such as Prozac and d-fenfluramine in damping down negative emotions, and the expansive, carefree mood produced by drugs of abuse that have mainly serotonergic affinities.[6]

Given the key role of serotonin, it was natural that researchers would look for variation in the genes that produce it and its associated proteins. There are two forms—short and long—of the gene that makes the chemical whose function it is to remove serotonin from the synapse between neurons (the 'serotonin transporter gene'). Sure enough,

Klaus-Peter Lesch and his colleagues found that people with at least one copy of the short form had higher levels of Neuroticism than people with the long forms. This result has now been replicated a number of times. Once again, it is not found in all studies. The effect is small, and easily obscured by complex interactions between multiple genes, and between genes and the environment. However, the balance of evidence points to a role for variation in the serotonin transporter gene in Neuroticism. A new type of evidence has recently added weight to this view. This is the combination of brain imaging with molecular genetics. Participants with the short form of the gene show a greater increase in amygdala activation when presented with pictures of fearful faces than do people with the long form.[7]

Neuroticism will no doubt turn out to be affected by multiple genes, and a network of different brain areas, but we can say with some confidence that the completion of that particular puzzle is underway. Let us now go back to the nature and consequences of Neuroticism at the psychological level.

The most obvious indicator of high Neuroticism in Susan's story is her bouts of clinical depression. Neuroticism is not just a risk factor for depression. It is so closely associated with it that it is hard to see them as completely distinct. It is true that Neuroticism is a stable and enduring trait, whilst depression is a disease state that may be considered present at some times and not at others. However, depression tends to be recurrent. A person who has had one episode has a 50 per cent chance of having another within two years, and an 80 per cent chance of having another at some point. Moreover, even when the full-blown condition is in remission, people who suffer from depression show definite hallmarks in their emotional style. It is thus probably better to think of depression as the periodic, often reactive, flare-up of the effects of the underlying personality trait, rather than something that comes out of the blue and then goes away entirely. Depression can be thought of as that state where the negative emotions—especially sadness, if the depression is of melancholy type—become so aroused that they self-perpetuate, at least for a while, and, clearly, the more reactive they are, the more likely they are to hit that state from time to time.[8]

People often ask me whether depression is due to the person or the situation they are in. This makes no more sense than asking whether flooding is due to the height of the water or the height of the land. There is no doubt that depression is often precipitated by life events. It may well be the case that anyone could become depressed. However, some people would require huge stressors, and others, much smaller ones. Neuroticism predicts the size of one's negative response to a daily hassle, and also the size of one's response to a more serious threat. Very high scorers can be pushed under by threats that would be brushed off or not even noticed by low scorers. Thus, high scorers live on low ground, and only a small increase in water levels are required to flood them.

An interesting genetic study by Avshalom Caspi and colleagues has recently shed light on how this differential vulnerability works. The researchers divided a large group of young New Zealand adults whose mental health had been followed over time into three groups, based on their genotype. The groups consisted of individuals with two copies of short forms of the serotonin transporter gene (s/s), one short and one long copy (s/l; remember we get one copy from each parent, and so there is no reason they should be the same), and two copies of long forms (l/l). The participants were interviewed, and the researchers rated whether they had had none, one, two, three or four or more of a series of really stressful life events over a five-year period. The life events were major problems or negative turns in housing, health, employment, relationships, and so on.[9]

Amongst those who had had no negative life events, rates of depression were uniformly low, regardless of genotype. In general, the more life events people had, the more likely they were to have had a problem with depression. However, the gradient of the relationship was not the same for the three genotypes. For the l/l group, the rate of depression was under 20 per cent even when four or more negative life events had occurred. For the s/s group, the rate of depression was 20 per cent with two life events, around 30 per cent with three, and over 40 per cent with four or more. The s/l group were intermediate between the two others; more vulnerable to depression for a given level of life stress than l/l, but less than s/s. This study is the clearest demonstration yet that our inherited temperament determines the magnitude of our reaction to negative events, and that depression is the result of an interaction between our own make-up (the height of the land), and the things that happen to us (the height of the sea).

Depression is not the only disorder related to Neuroticism. There is a large group of disorders which have distinct names but which in practice tend to overlap with each other and with depression and occur in the same people: anxiety disorders, phobias, eating disorders, post-traumatic stress disorders, obsessive-compulsive disorder. All of these are characterized by heightened Neuroticism. The difference between them may be due to other personality factors and individual differences, but their common core of distress is related to Neuroticism. For example, the melancholy type of depression is particularly likely if the person is also low in Extraversion, whilst this is not the case for anxiety disorder. In addition, several personality disorders, and even schizophrenia, are linked to high Neuroticism, as are other types of problem such as insomnia and headaches.[10]

The 'Neuroticism-as-negative-emotion' account I have given so far makes partial sense of Susan's story. She certainly

expresses plenty of negative emotions in her writing. She
was 'petrified' starting school; 'painfully shy' as a child. Her
extreme intelligence, which led to her skipping two years and
going to an out-of-district private school on a scholarship was
not a source of joy or pride. It was, she says, 'the final nail
in my coffin'. 'I hated playtime', she goes on, 'I . . . became
adept at 'being ill''; and, later, 'I hated school and started
being sick every morning just at the thought of it'. You get
a lot of first-person pronouns in Susan's account, often coupled with verbs of suffering. This is typical of high-scorers'
writing.[11]

There is a paradox about Susan, though, given what I have
said. If Neuroticism makes us hypervigilant to cues of threat
in the environment, how on earth did she end up coupled
with a spouse-abuser, a philanderer, and a drinker? Surely, her
psychological warning systems should have been twitching at
the slightest cue of these kinds of problems, and she should,
by the logic of negative emotions, have stayed a mile clear, or
at least got out very soon. Why did she not do so?

To understand this we need to address a further aspect
of Neuroticism, which is that negative emotion is very often
directed towards the self. The mechanisms we use to assess
ourselves and our own worth are just as affected by negative
emotion as those we use to assess the external world. I am
sure Susan did pick up on the cues of trouble with those
men, and I bet she lay awake worrying about them. But

being alone may have been equally terrifying, and her own self-esteem may have been too low to think she could do any better. After all, despite being the brightest pupil her school had ever had, she would not put herself forward for university or art college. This is not the behaviour of someone who has faith in herself.

Coupled with low self-esteem is instability in the self-concept. The high Neuroticism scorer is constantly ruminating, wondering whether she has done the right thing in life. Presumably one of the dangers our negative emotions are designed to detect is the danger of taking the wrong path in life, and so when the negative emotions are active, we will constantly doubt this. Susan, like many of my high-Neuroticism correspondents, reports several changes of identity and goals, continuing well into mature life: 'I often wondered whether I was doing the right thing in life'. Such correspondents often begin their accounts by saying how grateful they are for this opportunity to reflect on their lives, and try to sort out for themselves what they are trying to do. Low scorers don't say this; they know what they are trying to do, and they probably write for my benefit rather than their own. The high scorers can write a lot, too, perhaps because I have given them a licence to ruminate.

Instability in personal identity finds its height in a condition called borderline personality disorder. I am not suggesting that Susan has this condition. However, it is characterized by extremely high Neuroticism. Its main symptoms are instability in life arrangements and in personal goals, coupled with a chronic feeling of worthlessness or emptiness. Sufferers take on many new life plans, often unrealistic, and make many short-term marriages, often unsuitable. They seem to do this as a consequence of chronic doubt about who they are, what could make them happy, and what they are really worth. In Robert McCrae and Paul Costa's insightful phrase, the high Neuroticism scorer, 'keeps trying new self-definitions, like an insomniac who cannot find a comfortable position in bed'.[12]

Unstable self-definitions and low self-esteem contribute to perhaps the cruellest feature of Neuroticism, which is that the worried actually have more to worry about than the carefree. Study after study has shown that not only do high scorers react more strongly to negative life events; they have more negative life events to react to. There are a number of factors that may lie behind this association, though it is not entirely understood. For one thing, since Neuroticism is heritable and runs in families, the biological family members of high scorers are much more prone than average to depression, suicide, and other types of suffering that may affect their kin. Moreover, the low self-esteem of the high scorer may lead them to resorting to things with a higher than fair probability of going awry. One thinks of Susan's insisting on marrying the 'drunk and penniless' Steven, to the amazement of her colleagues. Many decisions taken in desperation to alleviate negative emotion may not be very wise ones. Finally, negative emotion can bring about the very behaviour it seeks to avoid. The man who constantly worries and nags his partner due to fear of her leaving may be giving her reason to do so.

There seem to be a litany of woes awaiting the high Neuroticism scorer. Let us just recap what they are. High scorers have increased rates of depression, anxiety disorders, insomnia, and stress-related problems of all kinds. High scorers visit their doctors more than low scorers, and rate their health as worse. In the very long term, they seem to have a slightly increased risk for all kinds of disorders, from heart disease to gastric disorders and including, perhaps unsurprisingly, hypertension. They may also have poorer immune functioning, a consequence no doubt of the immunosuppressant effects of chronic elevation in stress hormones. Outside the health sphere, other costs include less satisfactory marriages, less satisfaction at work, and a greater feeling that others are out to get them.[13]

The thesis of this book is that all personality traits bring benefits as well as costs, and Neuroticism looks like being the toughest case to argue. Neuroticism looks simply miserable, pathological even. However, I do not believe this is the case, and I will spend the rest of the chapter outlining some fragments of evidence for my position.

The first thing to point out is that the negative emotions are clearly there for a reason. They are protective systems for our body and mind, and it would be disastrous to lack them entirely. There are occasional cases of congenital inability to feel physical pain, and those with this condition always die very young through an inability to detect things that are damaging them. Similarly, the damage to the extremities associated with the disease of leprosy is actually a consequence of the loss of feeling. Sufferers cannot tell when they are damaging their hands. The loss of the ability to feel pain has a terrible cost, and the same is surely true of fear, sadness, and guilt.[14]

Given that we must have the negative emotions, the question is where their threshold should be set. As in the smoke-alarm example, making them more responsive will lead to more false alarms, but will also ensure that real threats are not missed. Recall the guppy example from Chapter 2. Guppies which were insufficiently anxious in an environment containing a predator were likely to end up inside the said predator. The most anxious guppies bore a cost—I think of their reduced feeding and greater vigilance as similar to an anxiety disorder in humans—but they would be more likely to leave descendants. In fact, under ancestral conditions, very low Neuroticism scorers amongst humans would plausibly suffer increased mortality from predation. This is a very hard prediction to test, of course, but I am prepared to bet it is true. There might be subtle, related effects still at work in modern society, though, as we shall see.

One way to approach this issue is to look at groups who have been identified as low Neuroticism scorers. One such group is climbers of Mount Everest. Sean Egan was at Everest base camp in the spring of 2000, where large numbers of climbers had assembled and were waiting to attempt the summit. In a stunning display of high-altitude personality research (17,600 ft. above sea level), he had thirty-nine climbers complete questionnaires. The climbers score much lower on Neuroticism than general population samples; around one standard deviation lower, in fact, which is a big difference. (They are high in Extraversion, too.) That people attempting this dangerous feat would report themselves as low in anxiety and good at coping with stressful situations is not, perhaps, surprising. However, it is suggestive of the dangers of low Neuroticism. Around 300 climbers have died on Everest. We don't know how many have attempted it, though around 1000 have made it to the summit. If we liberally assume that around one in three attempts is successful, that would mean 3000 people had tried, of whom 300 had died in the process, a mortality rate of one in ten. Climbing Everest is a very dangerous thing to do.[15]

Whilst one might admire the courage of these climbers, then, their low Neuroticism is making them ignore very real threats to their lives. Similarly, low Neuroticism is thought to be ideal for police and military work, professions also distinguished, unfortunately, by relatively high mortality rates. People very low in Neuroticism may, in virtue of their personalities, fail to avoid danger. There is a suggestion that people who are predatorily aggressive and break social rules can be low in Neuroticism, presumably because our fear of sanction is one of the factors restraining us from such behaviours. Some writers have also argued that 'the successful psychopath'—i.e. the remorseless, glib, untruthful exploiter—is low in Neuroticism, having no fear of the consequences of his actions. In such cases, low Neuroticism is clearly not a sufficient condition for antisocial behaviour to result. Everest climbers are low in Neuroticism but there is no reason to believe they are an antisocial lot. I will argue later that there are tripartite restraints on immoral behaviour—fear of the consequences, deliberation, and empathy for others. Low Neuroticism would only remove the first of these. A person would have to be low on Agreeableness and low on Conscientiousness as well to have all three restraints down.[16]

In the ancestral environment, then, it is quite plausible to argue that too low Neuroticism would have been selected against, because of the increased mortality it caused. When conditions were harsh and there were real threats from intra- and inter-group competition, those highest in Neuroticism may have done well. 'Just because I am paranoid', Israeli Prime Minister Golda Meir is reputed to have said, 'doesn't mean they're not out to get me'. On the other hand, when conditions were beneficent, high scorers would have paid the cost of all that worry, and lost out relative to the carefree souls who just got on with life. Once again, the optimal level would plausibly fluctuate with local conditions and composition of the surrounding population.

These benefits of Neuroticism in terms of reduced predation and mortality are probably pretty remote for most readers (I, for example, have simply lost track of when I was last attacked by a large predator). So are there any benefits of Neuroticism which are actually useful in today's societies?

This is an interesting question, since although the outcomes of mood disorder are on average very negative—for example, for one's career—there are an extraordinary number of very high achievers who have suffered it, so at least some people high in Neuroticism must be doing well by it. Studies of writers, poets, and artists show that these groups have extremely high rates of depression, suggesting very high Neuroticism. Could their Neuroticism be helping them to achieve as they do?[17]

There are several ways it might help. First, they may write as a form of therapy. This may be true, but they would still have to write something other people wanted to read. For this reason, high Neuroticism is not sufficient to be a creative writer. You need to be high in Openness too (see Chapter 7), and probably have further qualities as well.

Second, high-Neuroticism scorers feel that things (and this applies to both the things in the world, and things inside themselves) are not all right as they are, and so they want to change them. Thus you would predict that high scorers would actually be innovators in various domains, particularly those concerned with understanding the self and giving it meaning. Related to this, high scorers are afraid of failing, and this—as long as they don't feel so awful that they can't function—motivates them to strive. There is plenty of evidence for Neuroticism-related striving. Workaholics, especially those who feel driven to work, as opposed to those who do it for fun or social contact, tend to be high scorers. James McKenzie studied Neuroticism as a predictor of attainment amongst university students, and found that, amongst those students with high 'Ego strength', higher scorers got better academic results. 'Ego strength' measures organization and self-discipline, which would in big five terms come under Conscientiousness. Thus, the negative affect these students experience seems to have been fuel for greater work and attainment, as long as they were of the mindset to convert that fuel into motion. If they were too disorganized, or of course if their negative affect tipped them over the clinical edge, then their Neuroticism would hinder more than help them.[18]

These are motivational advantages of Neuroticism. There may be cognitive ones too. It has long been known that, on average, people are over-optimistic about the outcomes of their behaviour, especially once they have a plan, and don't reflect particularly deeply on possible consequences. This is well documented in the business world, with its over-optimistic growth plans, and also in military leadership, where it is clear that generals are routinely over-sanguine about their likely progress and under-reflective about the complexities.[19]

Social psychologist Shelley Taylor has argued that this over-confidence is useful, particularly so once we are in the 'implementational' phase of whatever goal it is we are pursuing. Our rose-tinted glasses give us the courage and enthusiasm to press on with securing our objectives. But we don't always want to be in the 'implementational' phase, in case the goal we are implementing is an unwise one. We need to also visit the 'deliberational' phase, where we honestly and coldly review our situation, and change, abandon, or scale back plans if need be. In this phase, we feel less upbeat, we are more cautious, pay more attention to detail, and we worry and ruminate more.[20]

High-Neuroticism scorers visit this reflective mindset much more often than low scorers. There are some tasks involving predicting one's own future, or one's degree of control over the environment, where healthy volunteers are way too optimistic, and depressed patients see things more or less accurately. The healthy subjects are so caught up in their implementational strategies that they don't see things as they are. I wouldn't want to pursue this 'depressive realism' too far, since depressed people clearly hold some very distorted negative beliefs and interpretations. Nonetheless, there is a sense that the neurotic temperament provides an eye that sees the problems of the world starkly, in all their equivocal complexity. Interestingly, in a large and influential review of the effects of personality on occupational success, Neuroticism was, to the researchers' surprise, a (weak) positive predictor of success for professional occupations. Professional occupations are those that mainly involve thinking, and it is illuminating that Neuroticism tended to be advantageous in these fields and not in, say, sales or manual labour.[21]

I am constantly impressed by how those with the greatest insights into the human condition seem to have been unhappy figures. The dramatist Henrik Ibsen is a wonderful example. He even writes the trade-off between the overoptimism and depressive realism into one of his plays. In *Peer Gynt*, the Troll King offers Peer an eternal life without worry, in which he will be happy living in a parochial mountain pass, and think his life and marriage perfect. What does Peer have to give up in order to achieve this contentment? He has to have one eye plucked out, and the other altered so that it only sees in pink. To take the path of unreflective happiness, Peer must become unable to see the world for what it is, and give up striving for more. There are many niches in modern life, then, where the sober, critical eye is a valuable and important one. We don't, as a society, need everyone to be jolly and gung-ho all the time, just as, as individuals, we need to live in both the implementational and deliberational mindsets.

Psychiatrist Randolph Nesse has written interestingly about the excessive optimism of stock markets in the late 1990s. Investors ploughed more and more money into investments and companies, expecting double-digit returns to go on forever. They were partly whipped up by boundlessly optimistic brokers. It's true that all previous booms have been followed by a bust, they said, but this market is different. This market will go on rising forever. It didn't go on rising forever, needless to say, and a lot of people lost a lot of money. Nesse estimates that the proportion of Wall Street brokers taking Prozac or related antidepressants could have been as high as one quarter at this time, since these drugs had become widely available and accepted amongst urban professionals. The effects of Prozac on non-depressed people are not dramatic, but it does detectably reduce negative emotions. Those rose-tinted brokers could have done with a little more worry about them.[22]

A case can thus be made that increasing Neuroticism brings potential benefits, both in evolutionary terms, and also in the modern context. High scorers should therefore not just wish their worry away, but, just like any other trait, understand the strength, sensitivity, striving, and insight that it may give them. There are niches in the world where these are very valuable. They do come at a cost, though, of often awful suffering perfused through many days of their lived experience. Clearly, the art is to manage these costs, to live with them, and to limit them so they do not become overwhelming. Fortunately, there are ways of doing this, to which we return in Chapter 9.

5

Controllers

Imagine you are playing a card game, for money. There are four decks of cards face down on the table in front of you. You pick up cards in turn from whichever deck you want. Every time you do so, you get a cash sum. Sometimes, though, depending on the card you pick, you also have to pay a fine. The fine can be larger than the reward, so on the draws where you pay a fine, you will end up worse off than before.

Over time, you begin to notice that the reward for drawing a card from either of the left-hand two decks, call them A and B, is always $100, whereas the reward for drawing cards from decks C and D, the right-hand two, is only ever $50. This makes A and B look pretty attractive. However, in deck A, every now and then—every tenth card, on average—you hit a fine of $1250. In deck B, the fine is a little lower—$500—but you hit it every fourth card on average. For decks C and D, the fines are $250 every tenth card, and $100 every fourth card, respectively.

Which deck should you draw from? You can work out fairly easily which are going to be profitable and which not. For deck A, over ten draws you would receive ten times one hundred dollars, or $1000, in rewards. However, you would also hit an average of one $1250 fine. Thus, you would expect to be $250 worse off than when you started. A similar calculation applies to deck B. You would receive the same thousand dollars in reward, and hit an expected two-and-a-half fines of $500 dollars each. Since two-and-a-half times five hundred is also twelve hundred and fifty, the expected pay-off for deck B is the same as that of deck A—a net loss of $250.

Now consider the other two decks. Playing from C, you would receive only $500 in reward for ten draws. However, you would expect only a single $250 fine. Thus, deck C leaves you an expected $250 better off than at the outset. Deck D, as you can easily verify, leaves you in exactly the same position on average—that is, richer than when you began.

This scenario is called the Iowa gambling task. Its name is no reflection on either the rationality or the moral character of the fine folk of Des Moines, but the product of the simple accident that the researchers who invented it worked in that state at the time. Volunteer participants who play the game experiment with the different decks for a while, since they have not been told the rules explicitly and have to figure them out by trial and error, but after hitting a few fines in decks A and B, they start to avoid those loss-making decks in favour of the more profitable C and D. Over one hundred card draws, they will make significantly more from C and D than A and B.

Why is the Iowa a psychologically interesting task? It is interesting because A and B, the unprofitable decks, carry the largest immediate rewards. Drawing from A and B means one hundred dollars up front, whereas C and D mean only fifty. A and B are made unprofitable by the big fines lurking in them. However, you get the $100 reward every single time you play from them, and the fine much less often. So, in order to play the game profitably, you have to overcome the lure of the immediate $100 reward, in favour of the more deliberate consideration that you will be better off in the long run if you take the more modest pay-offs and much lower fines of C and D. Much of life has a character analogous to the Iowa task. I would probably get more immediate and guaranteed reward if I stopped working on this sunny afternoon (a public holiday, in fact), and went and played with my cat. I like playing with my cat. It reliably gives me pleasure. However, over the long run of life, I will obtain more good things if I inhibit the urge to take the immediate gratification, and continue writing this chapter instead. We are constantly inhibiting immediate rewards cued up in our environments, to follow instead some internally set goal or more deferred gratification.

Antoine Bechara and his colleagues developed the Iowa task to investigate a particular type of brain-damaged patient. It had been known for some time that when certain parts of the frontal lobe of the brain are damaged by a stroke or a head injury, previously cautious and upright individuals can become careless, impulsive, and sometimes follow socially inappropriate urges. For example, one man suffered a ruptured aneurysm that damaged the right orbitofrontal cortex of his brain. A previously responsible employee at a car plant, he now began taking cars off the company lot and driving them away, abandoning them near to his home. He soon lost this job, and struggled to hold down any subsequent one due to lack of punctuality and his joyriding habit. For many years, in periods of idleness, he would drink some alcohol and go out looking for a car to take and drive away. He abandoned the cars after a short ride, and never tried to profit financially from them. His general cognitive functioning was intact, and he knew that what he was doing was illegal. He just couldn't stop himself. He drove away around 100 cars, and served several spells in prison.[1]

The Iowa task confirmed the peculiar nature of the deficits of patients such as this. Their memory, language, and general intellectual functioning remains intact. However, they just can't stop playing decks A and B on the gambling task. Sometimes they even seem aware that what they are doing isn't going to be good for them, but they just can't seem to overcome the lure of that $100.[2]

The reason for discussing this task in a book about normal personality variation is that the tendency to choose decks A and B in the Iowa is not restricted to those who have had brain injuries. In fact, a diverse and illuminating set of non-brain-injured groups have shown up with the same pattern of performance. First up, and least surprising in a way, are problem gamblers. Gambling is big business in developed countries, and it is growing bigger all the time thanks to new forms such as spread betting and new media like the Internet. Up to 1 per cent of British people meet diagnostic criteria for problem gambling, which means not just that they gamble a lot, but that they cannot control their gambling, they endanger their well-being through it, and they pursue it to the exclusion of other reasonable goals in life. Problem gamblers choose disproportionately from decks A and B. Though they above all people should be able to work out the unfavourable returns, they can't stop themselves.[3]

Other groups with unusual Iowa performance are those who have, or have had, a dependency on alcohol, cocaine, or marijuana. These issues are even more common than problem gambling, and people affected by them also choose more cards from decks A and B in the Iowa task than volunteer controls. The effect is generally not as strong as that with

brain-injured patients, but it is reliably measurable. Interestingly, their performance is impaired even after they have
been 'dry' or substance-free for quite a long time, so the
immediate effects of their drug of choice are not the causal
factor. This raises the possibility that what predisposes some
people to form a dependency on a drug or, in the case of
gambling, a behaviour, is a personality trait that makes them
unable to stop themselves responding to a reward cue in the
environment.[4]

Iowa gambling-task performance is not the only thing
that pathological gambling and substance dependencies have
in common. These conditions are highly co-morbid, which
means that if you have one of them, you have a much greater
than average chance of having another one too. For example, Wendy Slutske and her colleagues investigated problem
behaviours in a cohort of around one thousand young adults
from New Zealand. Those with a dependence on cannabis
had a sixfold increase in their odds of having a dependence on
alcohol as well, compared to those with no cannabis dependency. Those dependent on alcohol had a fourfold increase in
the rate of nicotine dependence. Of those with problem gambling, two thirds also had a substance dependency. Problem
gambling was associated with more than threefold increases
in the rates of alcohol, cannabis, and nicotine addiction.[5]

Now it could simply be the case that the places where
lots of gambling gets done are also places where there

are lots of drink and drugs around, so the correlation between the behaviours is circumstantial rather than due to any deep characteristic of the people involved. This seems unlikely, however. Gambling and addictions coaggregate in families. This means that people who gamble show up among the biological relatives of people who drink (even if they themselves are not gamblers), and people who drink show up amongst the biological relatives of people who gamble. In the relatives of both, a condition called antisocial personality disorder appears at greater than chance frequency. Antisocial personality disorder is a rather broad label, and may actually describe a number of different personality configurations. In the relatives of gamblers and those with dependencies, the nub of the antisociality that shows up seems to be recurrent irresponsibility and law-breaking, rather like that of the man who borrowed cars.

Researchers have studied the co-occurrence of gambling, addictions, and antisocial behaviour in the population at large, within families, and using twins, and concluded that there is a genetic liability common to these kinds of uncontrolled behaviours. Thus, if drinking, drugs, gambling, and law-breaking occur in the same environments, it is probably not an accident of history. It reflects the temperamental make-up of the people drawn to these places. The significance of the Iowa gambling task is that it may point to what the key psychological variable in this temperament is. The person can't stop going for the big-paying decks A and B, even though they might know that it would be better for them not to. The link to law-breaking, gambling one's house away, and going back to the bottle is all too clear.[6]

The human population is not divided into two groups, those with an impulse control problem and those without. Instead, as with other personality characteristics, there is a long continuum, somewhere along which we each fall. In the five-factor model of personality, the dimension related to impulse control is called Conscientiousness. High scorers are disciplined, organized, and self-controlled, whereas low scorers are impulsive, spontaneous, and have weaknesses of the will.

Hold on, I hear you say. Surely the degree to which one will be tempted by things like drink and drugs is a matter of Extraversion. After all, I argued in Chapter 3 that Extraversion was a measure of the responsiveness of the brain reward systems that fire off in response to thrilling stimuli, and drink, drugs, and gambling are all thrills. This much is true. The really addictive drugs of abuse generate activity in the brain reward area, the nucleus accumbens, whose activity is especially associated with Extraversion. Yet in studies of which personality characteristics predict the development of addiction problems, it is Conscientiousness rather than Extraversion which features.[7]

To solve this puzzle, you have to distinguish between the reasons for starting something, and the reasons for not being able to stop. High-Extraversion scorers will get a bigger buzz from a drink, a high, or a thrilling game of chance than low scorers, because of all the nucleus accumbens activity it will create. However, if they are also high in Conscientiousness, they will be able to decide not to do it again, however big the buzz was. They can make this decision because they need to work the next day, or save up money for a parachuting trip that will be an even bigger buzz, or whatever. The point is that there are brain mechanisms whose function is to inhibit a response, however rewarding, that is being cued by the environment, in favour of some other goal or norm that the person holds and which is more important. If these control mechanisms are potent, the person will be highly conscientious, and if they are relatively weak, the person will be impulsive.

Addictions are really about the failure to inhibit a once-rewarded behaviour, not about the degree of euphoria that is created. In many addicts, the pleasure achieved from the fix is essentially zero, since their brains have become so used to the addicted substance. The reasons for relapse are not pleasure-seeking or even craving so much as the inability of inhibitory mechanisms to stop the habit once formed.[8]

As we saw earlier, the Iowa gambling task was developed to investigate mental functioning in patients with injuries

in the frontal lobe of the brain. The particular pattern
of problems those patients have tells us that the frontal
lobes are important in these Conscientiousness-type control
mechanisms. Brain imaging allows us to refine this gener-
alization. We know, for example, that when a volunteer is
engaged in the Iowa gambling task, dorsolateral prefrontal
and orbitofrontal brain areas are metabolically active. Impulsive participants, or patients with impulse-control disorders
such as addictions, show relatively lowered activity in the
dorsolateral prefrontal, anterior cingulate, and orbitofrontal
cortices, particularly of the right hemisphere of the brain,
when engaged in the Iowa or similar tasks. This relatively
weak mobilization of frontal lobe response is thought to lie
behind the participant's poor performance.[9]

Let us look at one brain-imaging study in some more
detail. Shuji Asahi and his colleagues at Hiroshima University
scanned volunteers' brains using fMRI whilst the volunteers
did what is known as a Go-No Go task. In such a task, you
have to press a key as fast as possible every time a letter
appears on a screen, except when that letter is an X, when you
have to do nothing. You soon get into the habit of responding
quickly as soon as something flashes up, and it is quite effortful to override the immediate response when an X appears.
You quite often make errors of commission, meaning you
press the button when the letter is an X and you should have
stayed still.[10]

When an X appeared, the participants showed an increase in brain activity in, among other areas, the right dorsolateral prefrontal cortex. Thus this area seems to be involved in inhibiting the response to the environmental cue (a letter appearing) with the person's internally held rule (if it is an X, don't respond). Even more interestingly, the magnitude of the increase in brain activity in this region was linearly related to the person's score on a personality scale that they had filled in before the experiment. The scale measured impulsiveness, which we can think of as the inverse of Conscientiousness. Those who were the least impulsive (most conscientious) had the largest right dorsolateral prefrontal activation when they had to inhibit the key-press. The implication seems to be clear; Conscientiousness is the magnitude of reactivity of those mechanisms in the frontal lobe that serve to inhibit an immediate response in favour of a goal or rule.

Very low Conscientiousness, then, means an addictive personality that can't stop doing things even when they are damaging. Most low scorers are not so extreme as to develop an addiction or an antisocial personality disorder, though. However, you can see milder traces of that difficulty with impulse control in all relatively low scorers. Several of my correspondents with fairly low Conscientiousness scores write about being ambitious but 'struggling with laziness', or else needing to advance their careers for financial reasons but wishing they didn't have to, since they naturally have a 'lack of focus', and would prefer to potter around. Work is the major domain where mildly low Conscientiousness has an impact. Conscientiousness is the most reliable personality predictor of occupational success across the board (as opposed to the personality requirements of particular types of job). In general, the higher Conscientiousness score you have, the better you will do, other things being equal.

The correlation between occupational success and Conscientiousness is not especially strong—around 0.2—indicating that many other factors have an influence. However, what is impressive is the sheer consistency of the findings. Across dozens of studies, the correlation shows up more or less identically whether the criteria for occupational success is ratings of job proficiency, speed of promotion, income, or success in completing training. Similarly, the correlation is found among professionals, managers, salespeople, police officers, and more routine occupations, so it cannot be put down to the specific demands of any one job type. The more conscientious you are, the better you will do in the workplace, however better is defined and whichever workplace it is.[11]

There are some hints as to why this should be the case. The benefits of Conscientiousness are especially evident when the worker has a lot of autonomy. This makes sense. If Conscientiousness is the ability to follow internally set goals or plans, then it is going to be relatively useful when nobody else is telling you what to do next. Moreover, studies within work environments show that high-Conscientiousness scorers set a lot of goals and stick to them, compared to low scorers, who set goals less often, and are also inclined not to stick to them. Low scorers procrastinate and put things off, which is a way of not executing goals.[12]

When I talk about Conscientiousness, people often respond by saying 'what you are describing just sounds like intelligence'. People who set goals and follow them, and avoid bad decisions, are just smart. This is reinforced by the feeling that frontal lobe inhibitory mechanisms, whose functioning I have argued to be the essence of Conscientiousness, sound like 'higher', sophisticated, cognitive functions which are close to a lay person's definition of intelligent behaviour.

This view is really a misunderstanding of what psychologists mean by intelligence. Patients with orbitofrontal damage can become impulsive without loss of general intellectual ability. Many very smart people can develop addictions. This is because intelligence is not to do with the functioning of any one set of mental mechanisms. Rather, it is a global measure of how well—how fast, how efficiently—our whole nervous system is working. Thus, in someone with a high IQ score, everything works efficiently, from basic reflexes, to motor skills, language, memory, the reward system, and the inhibitory system. This says nothing about the *relative* strength of those different systems in that person, and therefore makes no predictions about the level of Conscientiousness.

Or so I used to think. This clarification of the nature of intelligence predicts that there will be no relationship at all between personality and intelligence, but research in the last decade has shown that this is not quite true. There are no very *strong* relationships between personality and intelligence, but some relationships there are, though debate about their nature and significance goes on. Most strikingly, though, in a couple of studies where relationships between Conscientiousness and intelligence have been found, they are not, as you might imagine, positive, but weakly negative. The smarter people are, the less conscientious they are.[13]

The most likely explanation for this is that people who are very sharp soon learn that they can get away with not preparing things too much in advance, not being overly disciplined with their time, and so on, since their quick abilities will get them through whatever academic and professional challenges they meet. Conversely, people who are not quite so quick have to use organization and discipline to achieve what some others might achieve carelessly. Thus, a behavioural style is developed that compensates for the level of intelligence, and so ends up inversely related to it. This means that there is no intrinsic genetic connection between low Conscientiousness and high intelligence. Rather, the weak negative correlation is something that emerges through development.

Conscientiousness looks like an unmitigated good. It helps you avoid costly addictions and stay inside the law. It helps you succeed in your career. It also helps you live a long life, as we saw in Chapter 2. Surely, then, the more conscientious you are, the better, and in so much as natural selection has operated on the distribution of Conscientiousness, it would have always selected for higher and higher levels of the trait.

As you may imagine, I don't see things this way. For a start, the usefulness of Conscientiousness is something that is exaggerated by the contemporary developed-world environment. Our workplaces are very artificial ecologies. Few of our ancestors survived and reproduced by being able to stay in the same place for eight hours a day, quietly getting on with a series of pre-planned or repetitive tasks according to an explicit set of rules or norms. It is only the extraordinary differentiation and specialization of the modern economy that has generated the prolonged periods of doing just this that modern work and schools represent.

We have seen that Conscientiousness is about sticking to an internally held norm or plan. For a hunter-gatherer ancestor, it would of course have been useful to make plans and be able to follow them through. It might be very advantageous to carefully and deliberately develop skills in tool-making, a development whose pay-off might be years away, rather than just try to use whatever can be grabbed when a tool is needed. However, it would be easy to be overly conscientious. Much of hunter-gatherer life is unplannable because of events. It would really not be a good response, observing a passing herd of wildebeest, to say, 'Actually, Wednesday is my honey-gathering day'. Life for a hunter-gatherer would be a series of urgent improvisations on the stimuli occurring right now, be they passing prey, the lack of passing prey, attacks by others, changes in the make-up of the group, or countless other possibilities. People would do well who could abandon plans at a moment's notice and quickly mobilize an energetic, spontaneous, physical response to whatever happened to turn up.

In this context, I often think of how attention-deficit hyperactivity (ADHD), which we now call a disorder, might well have been a strength. ADHD is relevant to the current theme because young people with the condition are characterized by low Conscientiousness, as well as elevated Neuroticism, and, to a lesser extent, low Agreeableness. The other distinguishing feature is their sex: cases among boys outnumber those among girls by around 5 to 1. Affected individuals struggle to sit still in a classroom or workplace, and their impulsivity frequently gets them into trouble with bosses, teachers, and with the law. However, they do respond, strongly, spontaneously, and energetically, to immediate stimuli. There are some notable examples of ADHD lads who have gone on to do well in professional sports. In a hunter-gatherer world that is unpredictable, slightly lawless,

occasionally violent, physically active, and always changing, I
am sure many such boys would have fared extremely well.[14]

The story so far seems to suggest that Conscientiousness
could have been too high in the environment of our ancestors, but that in the context of modernity, Conscientiousness
brings only benefits. Even this is not true. There is a psychiatric diagnosis called obsessive-compulsive personality disorder, which represents high Conscientiousness in an extreme
form. Around 2 per cent of all adults meet the criteria for
receiving this diagnosis, and, as with any personality disorder, for every full-blown case, there are many others who
don't quite pass the diagnostic threshold, but are nonetheless
affected by some of the symptoms. Around twice as many
men as women are diagnosed with obsessive-compulsive personality disorder.[15]

Obsessive-compulsive personality disorder (OCPD) is
unhelpfully named, since it is not particularly closely related
to the better known obsessive-compulsive disorder (OCD).
It does not tend to co-occur with obsessive-compulsive
disorder, or even run in the same families. Obsessive-
compulsive disorder is an anxiety disorder, in which the
sufferer feels compelled to repeat particular thoughts or
actions, such as checking or hand-washing. As an anxious
condition, it belongs to the same family as depression and
generalized anxiety disorder, and thus is related to high
Neuroticism and responds to some extent to serotonergic

antidepressant medications. Some people have even seen obsessive-compulsive disorder as a *low* Conscientiousness problem, since the affected individual cannot inhibit the checking or washing response in rather the same manner as the alcoholic cannot inhibit his desire to drink. Whether this is the right characterization or not, it is clear that OCPD is a very different type of problem.[16]

What, then, does OCPD entail? Psychiatrists define it as 'a pervasive pattern of preoccupation with orderliness, perfectionism, and mental and interpersonal control, at the expense of flexibility, openness and efficiency, beginning by early adulthood and present in a variety of contexts'. I will illustrate some of the ways that such a pattern can surface by drawing on a clinical case study, that of Ronald, given in a well-known abnormal psychology textbook.[17]

People with OCPD are preoccupied with rules, lists, schedules, and all the other paraphernalia of keeping to an internally held plan. Ronald, for example, rises unvaryingly at 6.47 a.m. on weekdays, has two eggs soft-boiled for 2 minutes 45 seconds, and is at his desk at 8.15 a.m. The rest of his day goes on in a similarly regimented manner. He has separate Saturday and Sunday schedules. If these are forced to vary, he feels 'anxiety, annoyance, and a sense that he is doing something wrong and wasting time'. What is striking in OCPD is the disjunction between means and ends. Sticking to the schedule or plan becomes the main issue, and the actual point of the activity (e.g. to get fed, have a nice day, to bond, to achieve something) is entirely lost.

A second characteristic of OCPD is a perfectionism so great that it prevents the person getting things done. Ronald 'is highly valued at work because his attention to detail has, at times, saved the company considerable embarrassment'. However, his perfectionism also means that 'he is the slowest worker in the office, and probably the least productive. He gets the details right but may fail to put them into perspective'. Many OCPD sufferers struggle to complete anything at all, given their excessive need for perfection.

Interpersonal relationships are badly affected by OCPD. Sufferers will not allow themselves any fun, leisure, or undirected social time. They are seen by others as grim and austere. They are also extremely scrupulous and inflexible in the application of their rules about right and wrong, to an extent that many others find tiresome, petty, and stubborn. Moreover, their need for order can make it hard to incorporate others into their daily routines. Ronald, for example, has 'a rather elaborate routine preceding his going to bed':

He must spray his sinuses, take two aspirin, straighten up the apartment, do thirty-five sit-ups and read two pages of the dictionary. The sheets must be of just the right crispness and temperature and the room must be noiseless. Obviously, a woman sleeping over interferes with his inner sanctum and, after sex, [Ronald] tries either to have the woman go home or sleep in the living room. No woman has put up with this for very long.

The damage OCPD does to interpersonal relationships, and thus to well-being and family life, is very clear. Sufferers may also be miserly and have an inability to throw anything away, so that their houses come to resemble meticulously ordered but useless hoards.

OCPD is a very isolating and distressing condition, but it is easy to understand in terms of the brain mechanisms of Conscientiousness we discussed earlier in the chapter. The frontal-lobe mechanisms that inhibit spontaneous responses in favour of internally generated rules or plans are so powerful in these people that there is no spontaneity at all. There are only rules or plans, and because of this, genuine, in the moment, interaction with others and with the environment becomes impossible, and so, valuable opportunities in social, romantic, professional, and experiential spheres simply go unseized. Thus, it really is possible to have too much Conscientiousness.

There is another way that excessive Conscientiousness can surface in women, and this is in disordered eating. Studies of anorexia nervosa have found that Neuroticism is elevated in this condition, which is no surprise, since Neuroticism is elevated in almost all psychiatric problems. However, perfectionism, which is just very high Conscientiousness, also surfaces as a recurrent feature. Moreover, anorexia can be co-morbid with OCPD, anorexia patients score high on checklists designed to assess OCPD, and the two disorders tend to run in the same families. Thus it seems that in anorexia, two separate effects occur, whose interaction is particularly dangerous. Young women high in Neuroticism will tend to have low self-esteem and negative feelings about their bodies. They thus try to control their food intake using frontal-lobe inhibitory mechanisms rather than responding spontaneously to food cues in their environment. If these frontal-lobe control mechanisms are very powerful, this strategy works all too well, and they end up starving themselves.[18]

Over evolutionary time, then, I expect that high Conscientiousness has sometimes been a curse and sometimes a blessing, depending on local conditions. Broadly, if the environment is very stable and predictable, so that you can know some time in advance what the best thing to be doing on a given day is, then high Conscientiousness would be selected for, as high-scoring individuals would be focused, organized, and not get distracted. On the other hand, if the environment is unpredictable, the people who will do best are those who can respond spontaneously to whatever it throws at them at that particular moment. High Conscientiousness scorers don't do well when you have to be this flexible, as they find the change of routine upsetting and difficult to adjust to.

When the environment is very unpredictable and fluid, low Conscientiousness scorers such as the young men nowadays characterized with ADHD might get on very well indeed. The broad spectrum of Conscientiousness we see today probably reflects the inconsistency of selection that humans have experienced in the past.

I don't have any examples as extreme as OCPD in the case studies I have gathered, but some of the problems as well as advantages of high Conscientiousness are detectable in one story in particular, and it is with this story that I shall end this chapter. Katherine grew up in a remote provincial city in Scotland, to parents who were doctors. She graduated from school with the maximum grades that it is possible to have (putting her in the top few per cent of academic attainment for her cohort), and, passing on to one of Scotland's finest universities, earned not one but two Bachelor's degrees over four years. She certainly worked hard. As she says:

I took on a masochistic amount of work ... which included part-time research jobs, teaching assistant position, part-time job marking exams, completing my dissertation, and the rest of my courses ... I completed 200 hours of volunteer work and served in elected offices for student organizations, including as Secretary and Treasurer of the voluntary organization I was part of.

What might explain this prodigious array of activity? Katherine says:

My work ethic is hypomanic: almost constantly, I am working on something, researching, thinking, planning, doing things. It is difficult to do nothing...If I take time to do nothing, I feel wasteful and lazy...I do not procrastinate on important things, and usually not on unimportant things either.

She describes her least favourite thing as 'wasting time not accomplishing anything' and 'feeling out of control'; and the tone of her life as 'serious, extremely driven...but not carefree or relaxed'; 'I feel pressured by myself to succeed'. All this makes for a very impressive *curriculum vitae*. I do sense, however, that this has not come without cost. Although she never sought treatment, she suspects she was anorexic and bulimic in school, and eating issues continue to be a concern. She mentions social acquaintances but few close friends, and only rather high-minded, improving hobbies. She has never, it seems, really had a satisfactory romantic relationship, and the rules she sets herself add up to a hard taskmaster:

I've spent a great deal of effort refining my personal philosophy and acting accordingly. At times, I want to do what my philosophy prohibits, and doing the right thing is very difficult.

Having graduated from university, and temporarily thwarted in her original plan to become a lawyer, Katherine seems to me slightly at a loss. I recognize this syndrome very well amongst highly academic, conscientious young people. The school-college-university ladder, with frequent exams and goals to work towards, gives them a set of targets to work towards. Spat out into the world, there is suddenly less clarity about what the next objective is, and this can be a very disorienting time. I would not imagine low-Conscientiousness students having a problem at this point. They just go travelling, or hang out, and something comes up sooner or later. I hope Katherine will find her next set of goals soon. She ends on an optimistic note, though, betokening a capacity to learn and an understanding of the hazards of her personality.

I have been so devoted to work in the past I have gone so far as to discredit the value of recreation and pleasure, but lately I have become more balanced and welcoming of pleasure.

Good for her.

6

Empathizers

Suppose for a moment you have been lured into a laboratory by a psychologist. You are seated in a small cubicle, with a clear glass front. You are hungry. Just opposite you, the other side of a narrow corridor, is someone you know. He looks like he is in the same boat as you. In front of you are two levers. One of them, you have worked out, will bring a tray that is currently out of reach into your reach though a gap in the glass wall. On that tray is a glass of chilled water and something nice to eat. The second lever will also bring your tray into your reach, and additionally cause a similar tray to be moved into the reach of the man opposite. If you can only pull one lever, which lever do you pull?

The answer seems incredibly obvious. Pulling the second lever leaves you exactly as well off as pulling the first, and in addition, and at no extra cost to yourself, helps out someone else who is in a similar plight to you. Of course that is the one that you would pull, and the overwhelming majority of other people would do the same. It seems the natural thing to do. But natural for whom? The interesting thing is that more or less this exact experiment has been done with chimpanzees, from three different captive populations, and there is no sign that they take any interest in the pay-off for the other individual. The chimps choose the best pay-off for themselves, and if two different levers give them the same pay-off, they choose between them randomly, without giving any weight at all to what happens to the other chimp.[1]

These experiments are all the more remarkable because the second chimp is one who is well known to the first, and lives in the same colony. In the human case, by contrast, we would not only choose the mutually beneficial lever when someone we know is in the opposite cubicle. Most of us would choose that lever when it was a complete stranger. This is part of the great mystery of human life that has been called, variously, pro-sociality or ultra-sociality. We give blood, we donate to charity, we return lost wallets, we give directions to strangers in the street. We leave tips in restaurants in distant cities that we can be sure we will never visit again. Why do we do this?

There are various classes of experiment that allow us to investigate this phenomenon further. In the so-called Dictator game, player A is given a sum of money, let us say $10, and told to divide it up in any way that they like between themselves and player B. The two players will then keep the money they have been allocated. From the point of view of narrow self-interest, player A should just give the minimum possible amount to B, and keep the rest for himself: $9 to $1, for example. This is almost never what happens. Even when the players are explicitly told that this is a one-shot situation with no opportunity for B to turn the tables, when the money is real, and when B is a stranger, players of the A role offer B substantial amounts, often 50 per cent. Numerous other experiments with different set-ups tell exactly the same story. The only way economists can make what people do in these situations seem like a rational choice is to assume that people have 'other-regarding preferences'. By this they mean that the utility or satisfaction person A gets from an outcome depends partly on what person B gets, as well as what they themselves get.

Other-regarding preferences, though pervasive, are an extremely puzzling aspect of human psychology. From a Darwinian point of view, we should not expect them to evolve unless some fairly unusual circumstances obtain. This is because natural selection is driven, to a reasonable approximation, by the differential reproductive success of individuals. It thus designs psychologies that make individuals good at looking after their own interests, not the interests of their competitors. (Close kin are an easily explicable exception, though interestingly some of the chimps in the experiments described above were siblings and half-siblings, and this didn't make any difference.)

In trying to explain why people have other-regarding preferences, it is important to distinguish the proximate from the ultimate story. The ultimate story concerns why natural selection favoured individuals with other-regarding preferences in the human lineage and in, as far as we know, no other primate and perhaps no other animal. This is an issue to which we will return later in the chapter. Whatever the ultimate story turns out to be, though, there is also a proximate question to be answered, namely, what psychological capacities make individuals behave in other-regarding ways? Here the answer seems pretty clear; other-regarding behaviour is linked to a broad umbrella of mental mechanisms known as 'theory of mind'. Theory of mind allows us to represent the mental state of another individual. Through theory of mind, we can appreciate that the individual in the cubicle opposite *feels* hungry, *wants* the food, *believes* that we should help to get food, and so on. In the chimp experiments, it is not that the chimps always chose the lever that would not reward the other individual instead of the lever that would. Rather, they simply weren't influenced either way by the outcome for the other chimp. It is as if they simply didn't compute the desires of the other individual at all, which squares with other evidence that chimpanzee theory of mind capacities are extremely rudimentary at best.[2]

Human theory of mind can be divided into two related capacities, mentalizing and empathizing. Mentalizing is what we do when we attribute a mental state such as a belief or desire to another person. Mentalizing is not available from birth. This was shown with a classic experiment using two puppets acting out a short scene. One puppet, Sally, has a basket. Sally puts a marble in her basket and then leaves the scene. Whilst Sally is away, the other puppet, Anne, moves the marble from the basket to a box. Sally then returns. The question for the participant is, 'where will Sally look for her marble?'

Children under four have no problem answering the question. Sally will look in the box. Why? Because that is where Anne has put it, of course. Children of four and up make the transition to seeing that Sally must look in the basket, because they can separate their own knowledge that the marble is in fact in the box from Sally's mental state, namely the (erroneous) belief that the marble is in the basket.[3]

Simon Baron-Cohen and his colleagues famously showed that autistic individuals were specifically impaired on this type of mentalizing. They struggle to represent the mental states of others, even if they are relatively unimpaired on other types of cognitive task. More recently, it has become clear that there is quite a lot of variation in mentalizing abilities amongst 'normal' adults, too. To demonstrate this, you need a very much harder task than the Sally-Anne, which all normal volunteers pass extremely easily. There are a variety of such tasks. One, devised by Peter Kinderman and colleagues, and later expanded by James Stiller and Robin Dunbar, asks participants to listen to rather complex stories with several characters in them, and then answer questions. Some of the questions tap factual memory for the events of the stories, to check the participant has been paying attention and provide a baseline. The others set difficult mentalizing problems about the characters. They exploit the fact that human mentalizing can be nested, so I can understand your beliefs, and I can also understand your beliefs about someone else's beliefs. I can even understand your beliefs about someone else's beliefs about a third person's beliefs, and so on.[4]

Studies using this task show that most people can go fairly comfortably to around fourth-level nesting. This means being sure whether statements like the following are true or not:

Tom hoped that Jim would believe that Susan thought that Edward wanted to marry Jenny.

Above this level it becomes dramatically more difficult to keep track. Try, for example:

John thought that Penny thought that Tom wanted Penny to find out whether Sheila believed that John knew what Susan wanted to do.

However, some people within normal volunteer populations do much better at this task than others, and it seems that the variation is meaningful. People who do well at this task have a larger network of friends than those who do less well, for example. Beth Liddle devised a version for school-age children, and showed that how well the children performed correlated strongly with teachers' ratings of how well they got on with their peers. Thus there is population variation in mentalizing abilities, and it seems to affect behavioural outcomes.[5]

The other aspect of theory of mind is empathizing. This also involves representing the mental state of others, but in the particular case where that mental state is an emotion. By empathizing with another's emotion, we are potentially affected by it too. Empathizing is what we do when we say, 'I can imagine how awful that felt'. Brain-imaging evidence suggests that empathizing makes use of several of the brain areas involved in mentalizing, plus additionally the brain areas that would be involved in actually having the relevant feeling at first hand. Thus mentalizing and empathizing capacities are clearly overlapping. However, as we shall see later, there may be some personality configurations where one is more implicated than the other.[6]

If theory of mind is the psychological capacity that underlies pro-social behaviour, and if there is variation in the population in theory of mind performance, then it obviously follows that there should be variation in the population in how pro-social people are. Experience reveals such variation all the time. Some people are always thinking of the needs of others, and go out of their way to be kind and fair. Others fail to attend to the needs or desires of those around them, and pursue their path with little thought given to anything beyond their own interests. Similarly, in games such as the Dictator game, not everyone's behaviour is the same.

The five-factor model of personality identifies, from rating data, a trait called Agreeableness. High scorers are described as cooperative, trusting, and empathetic, whilst low scorers are cold-hearted, hostile, and non-compliant. Though this is clearly a dimension of pro-sociality, curiously, no-one had made a link between Agreeableness and theory of mind until recently. I decided to investigate the correlation between the two. The first clue that there might be a relationship came from the fact that a measure called the empathy quotient turned out to be very highly correlated with Agreeableness from the five-factor model. The empathy quotient had been devised by Simon Baron-Cohen and his colleagues to assess variation in the theory of mind abilities that they study. However, the empathy quotient is a self-report questionnaire scale, just like Agreeableness is, and it would be more convincing to show a relationship between Agreeableness and a measure of theory of mind that does not depend so obviously on self-description. Beth Liddle and

I therefore decided to administer the Kinderman-Stiller stories task, described above, to sixty students, who would also fill in a five-factor personality questionnaire. We found an encouraging correlation—around 0.5—between Agreeableness score and score on the theory of mind questions about the stories. The correlation is not perfect, but it is way above chance.[7]

To be high in Agreeableness, then, is to be disposed to pay attention to the mental states of others, and, crucially, to factor these into behavioural choices. An ingenious recent experiment has shown that Agreeableness score predicts how much time people will spend processing words like 'caring', 'console', and 'help' compared to words like 'abduct', 'assault', and 'harass' when the words are presented on a screen in front of them. Such preferences produce prosocial, warm, trusting behaviour. People who score high in Agreeableness help others more, have harmonious interpersonal relationships, enjoy good social support, and relatively rarely fall out with or insult people. They are quick to forgive, and slow to anger, even with people who are in fact blameworthy.[8]

Let us take Maria, for example. Maria scored pretty much at the top of the Agreeableness scale. She is an associate professor in Latin American studies at a medium-sized university in Florida. She is clearly an outstanding young scholar, but her story tells more about her relationships with others than her personal achievements. Moving swiftly on from hints that she is the rising star of her department, she writes instead:

My personal relationships range from good to excellent, both in my marriage, my family (nuclear and extended), my in-laws, most colleagues at University and a variety of friends I have made during the years and whose loyalty and friendship I esteem highly.

In her office at the University, she is constantly interrupted by noise and callers, but whereas many academics would curse the distraction, Maria writes, 'I love the company and the relationships with my colleagues', and hints that she works in the department for this reason although she would get more done by working at home. Despite abundant evidence of good interpersonal relationships, including a family she sees nearly every day and a happy marriage, Maria feels that she has 'slightly neglected my loved ones...striving to be hyperproductive'. She has thus decided 'to continue being productive, but not at a rate that will estrange me from the people and the things that I love'. This trade-off, between relationships and personal advancement, is one to which we shall return.

As well as her close relationships and her work, Maria is involved in what she describes as 'a small number of activities that are pleasurable to me in a moral way'. These include volunteer work with Hispanic immigrants downtown, and donating blood. This idea of moral pleasure seems to me a powerful one that sums up the high-Agreeableness personality. Many of my correspondents who score high in Agreeableness are counsellors, or social workers, or involved in volunteer activities for the good of others.

If relationship orientation and moral pleasure are the signatures of the high-Agreeableness personality, then what is the low-Agreeableness personality like? We already know that such people will be less inclined to trust or help others, more inclined to be cold or antagonistic, have less harmonious interpersonal relations, and spend more time processing agentic, competitive words like 'assault' than mutualistic, collaborative words like 'console'. Lessened theory of mind processing has also been linked to paranoia. After all, if one does not accurately model the mental state of another, one may treat it as hostile.

One account from amongst those I have gathered illustrates these themes very clearly. I don't wish to give any biographical details, but some of the contrasts with Maria are instructive. Whereas Maria writes of her closeness to her family, this account tells of early years 'plagued with ... suspicion of my family'. The writer describes his parents as 'two very irresponsible idiots who had no business polluting the gene pool with their spawn, much less raising them'. His father was 'a spineless jealous little man-child' whilst his mother was 'lazy, weak, and stupid ... selfish, infantile, and most importantly duplicitous ... I cannot think of her in any way as good or trustworthy'. Regardless of what objective facts might be in this case, I have only ever encountered such hostile assessments of others in the accounts of those low in Agreeableness.

Whereas Maria takes moral pleasure in doing things to improve the lot of others, this account is more focused on extraordinary personal achievements; 'I can glimpse clips of myself in future performing great works, discovering revolutionary new ideas and, above all, being looked at in awe by my fellow inhabitants of Earth'. On the fact that others have viewed such an outlook as selfish, he states clearly:

I believe that this is just an attempt by those with substandard intellect to tear down my self-esteem. Why must we always give in to this idea of altruism when it comes to our unequals? It is ALWAYS, without a doubt, in my best interest to feel that I am more important than everyone else . . . Is that not what survival is?

What is interesting about this passage is that this person clearly does not have other-regarding preferences, or not to the same extent as Maria does. Logically, he is quite correct. From a Darwinian point of view, it is in general terms in an individual's best interest to rate his own (and perhaps his offspring's) welfare above that of everyone else. But given that humans are odd that way, it is quite rare to hear this value expressed so baldly. 'I do not care to help people', he says in another context, 'I feel no philanthropic love of humanity that drives me to fix its ailments'. Clearly, this account and Maria's moral pleasures are at the opposite ends of the spectrum, with the bulk of humanity falling somewhere in between.

At the very extreme low-Agreeableness end of the spectrum we find a condition called psychopathy. The psychopath is an individual who is completely egocentric, remorseless, dishonest, incapable of love, and disposed to use others entirely to forward his or her own ends. I am not suggesting that the person in the previous case study is in fact a psychopath. He is nowhere near that extreme. Not that I believe that psychopathy is an all-or-nothing phenomenon. There can obviously be degrees in psychopathy as in every other psychological characteristic. Nonetheless, the psychopathic cluster is clearly at the low-Agreeableness end of the spectrum.[9]

Many psychopaths are notorious criminals. They will often con, deceive, or manipulate people to gain resources, prestige, or gratification. They are also remarkable for their use of aggression. Not all aggression is a sign of psychopathy. People who are high in Neuroticism may be spontaneously aggressive under certain circumstances. As we have seen, such individuals have very active negative emotion systems, and these are likely to make them react strongly to something they perceive as a threat. The aggression of high Neuroticism, then, is always in reaction to a perceived threat or challenge, and may well be followed by remorse and regret once the panic has subsided. Psychopathic aggression is different. Psychopaths will use aggression instrumentally, to gain some end for themselves, with forethought, without provocation from the targeted party, and without remorse afterwards. The pain of the other party is simply given no weight whatever.

Not everyone with very low Agreeableness will be morally bad, or even necessarily hostile. Psychopathy is a complex constellation. The core seems to be lack of empathy, and this equates to very low Agreeableness. However, criminal psychopaths also tend to have low Conscientiousness, which will mean a certain lack of deliberation and control. They are often low in anxiety, too, which makes them fearless in going through with their schemes. There are three distinct psychological sources of restraint from immoral or antisocial behaviour. Empathy for others forms the first, perhaps the single most important one. Deliberation forms the second. When we think through the consequences of our action instead of responding directly, we often realize that we would do better in the long term by foregoing an immediate reward but gaining some larger deferred one. Fear is the third. If we trick or deceive someone else, they may find out and punish us, and our fear of that outcome deters us.

Each of these three restraints corresponds to the low pole of one of the big five personality dimensions. Someone very low in Agreeableness lacks empathy. However, deliberation or fear may still restrain him from antisocial behaviour. Someone low in Conscientiousness lacks deliberation, but empathy or fear may restrain him. Someone low in Neuroticism may have no fear, but be restrained by his empathy and deliberation. This tripartite system means, happily, that the odds are strongly stacked in favour of pro-social behaviour. Only when all three gates are open—very low Agreeableness, very low Conscientiousness, very low Neuroticism— is serious, callous, cruel psychopathic behaviour going to result. Even if one in fifty people had one of the 'open gates', then, assuming, as is not far from the truth, that scores on the big five are independent of one another, then only one in one hundred and twenty-five thousand would be at risk of becoming seriously bad. Reassuringly, this squares with everyday experience. Cases of torture or callous exploitation of one human being by another get so much press attention precisely because they are vanishingly rare and aberrant.[10]

I was keen to stress that low Agreeableness is not always related to hostility because there are, in my case studies, plenty of individuals who are certainly good citizens despite low Agreeableness scores. Back in Chapter 3, we met David, a research biochemist from Maryland who, being low in Extraversion, was relatively unmoved by career ambition and material success. David is also low in Agreeableness. Despite this, he is a reliable husband and father, and a competent teacher and colleague. However, he has also written with a disarming frankness about his orientation to other people. He is very interested in life, enjoying philosophy, science, and the countryside. He writes that 'A quiet sunny morning in the garden, observing flowers, insects, birds, animals, nature in general, is paradise for me.' However, he really isn't very interested in people. He describes his relationships as 'rather limited', and goes on:

I find human company rather boring most of the time. I prefer to be on my own, so that I have the freedom to let my thoughts go the way I want them to.

Whilst he admits that 'a lack of interest in other humans limits my ability to function well in human organizations', he says simply that he has 'no desire to improve on that', and indeed, why should he, since he is doing no-one any harm? Another passage is intriguing in its description of his experience of relationships:

In general, I avoid unnecessary complications. Interhuman relationships often fall into that category. They are full of hidden actions and signals of status and ranking contest, which irritate me and I prefer not to participate in.

That human interactions are full of status and ranking signals I do not dispute. What interests me is that David should find conversations to contain things that are 'hidden'. They would seem to be so to someone who does not focus very naturally on decoding the mental states underlying the words. Such a person would find conversation a complex and semi-opaque business.

This leads us naturally to the issue of autism. Autistic disorders are also distinguished by difficulties with theory of mind. Is there then some fundamental similarity between autism and psychopathy? Autistic individuals do have problems forming social relationships, and do get into trouble because of their difficulties relating to people, but the nature of the deficit seems somewhat different from that of psychopaths. The distinction between the mentalizing and the empathizing components of theory of mind becomes useful here. Autistic individuals struggle to predict the mental states of others, but when they see another in distress, they can respond physiologically in a relatively normal way. Thus, they fail to mentalize, but do empathize when they get very direct evidence of another's pain. Conversely, psychopaths can be reasonably good at predicting others' mental states. This is how they manipulate and deceive people so effectively. What is missing is the connection of the output of this mentalizing to the emotional system. They mentalize without empathy, and thus, though they are capable of computing mental states when they need to, they give them no weight in determining their behaviour.[11]

We don't yet know how completely empathizing and mentalizing can be teased apart, since they rely on overlapping brain networks, and many theory of mind tasks are clearly drawing on both. It seems that Agreeableness is closer to empathizing than mentalizing. That is, being low in Agreeableness is not about *not being able* to work out the mental states of others, as autism is. It is about not being particularly *caring* about the output of that computation. This would make sense of what Beth Liddle and I found in our research. Agreeableness correlated with performance on the stories task, but not with performance on another theory of mind task called the 'reading the mind in the eyes' test. In the latter task, participants are directly challenged to compute mental states, and low Agreeableness participants do fine. In the stories task, the participant listens to the stories in an undirected way, and questions subsequently probe which aspects they have attended to and remembered. The low Agreeableness participants retained less information about the mental states of the characters involved than the high Agreeableness participants did.[12]

If people high in Agreeableness have harmonious interpersonal relationships and good social support, then high Agreeableness is clearly a good thing, isn't it? The answer to this question depends what meaning of 'good' is intended. It is morally good to have people high in Agreeableness around, since they have other-regarding preferences and act on them.

However, it is not so obvious that being high in Agreeableness is always 'good' for an individual in terms of getting on in life, and, similarly, it is likely to be a mixed blessing in terms of that ultimate currency, Darwinian fitness.

Natural selection ultimately rewards behaviours that promote the individual's own material and reproductive interests relative to the interests of competitors. Under normal circumstances it penalizes doing things for the good of the species, or the group, since such acts by definition reduce the relative advantage of one's own lineage. Being high in Agreeableness—that is, taking account of others' interests as well as one's own—looks like an evolutionary aberration. This is why it is no surprise that our chimpanzee cousins show no interest in the welfare of others.

Why should the Darwinian aberration of human prosociality have come about? This is still not fully explained, but any answer must surely appeal to our ancestors living in small, long-lasting social groups performing collaborative tasks, where the benefit of membership was high, and the cost of being ostracized near fatal. Under such circumstances, it would pay to always be a good group member, and avoid at all costs getting any kind of reputation for antisociality. In other words, this situation produces the unusual selection pressure whereby there are strong *self-interest* benefits to being very attentive to the interests of *others*, because that makes you a valued and secure group player. Additionally, the existence of language in humans means that if we are unhelpful, people can share information about us through gossip. Such information transfer means that uncooperative behaviours have a knock-on effect not just for the future relationship with one individual, but with a whole community. All the more reason to be other-regarding.[13]

However, just how other-regarding is it optimal to be? There is clearly a continuum from a little bit other-regarding (say, my interests are worth 80 per cent and everyone else's 20 per cent), to strongly other-regarding (20 per cent to 80 per cent). I contend that the Agreeableness dimension is essentially the dimension of how other-regarding you are, with low scorers (like psychopaths) weighing others' interests close to zero, and high scorers (like Maria) weighting them pretty highly. For our ancestors, the logical extreme of high Agreeableness would never have been adaptive, for that extreme means weighing the interests of others at 100 per cent and of the self at zero. Such people would have been wonderful to have around, but they have left no descendants in the modern world, since they would never eat until everyone else had had their fill in a time when there was frequently insufficient to go around. The closest thing we see to such a configuration in modern populations is what is termed 'dependent personality disorder'. This is a rare syndrome characterized by such a high degree of Agreeableness that the person completely sacrifices their own needs, values, options, pleasures, and goals in order to serve the desires of others. At the other extreme, people with no pro-social tendencies have probably left few descendants too, since they would have been ostracized and avoided. So selection has favoured people somewhere in the middle.[14]

Nonetheless, variation in Agreeableness has been maintained. This is presumably because the optimum degree of other-orientation versus self-orientation would vary subtly with the local ecology. In an environment where protein is only to be had by building salmon weirs, which take a large group of people cooperating to construct and maintain, being a good collaborator would clearly pay. On the other hand, a time of abundant small game which could be hunted on one's own might favour the individualist. As humans changed their subsistence and social context, so the selective pressures on Agreeableness would tug it this way or that.

There is also a more specific reason why the rewards of Agreeableness would vary ceaselessly, and this reason is frequency-dependency. Frequency-dependency, as we saw in Chapter 2, is that situation where doing something is rewarded as long as it is rare, but penalized when it becomes very common. When evolutionary theorists have modelled the evolution of cooperative behaviour, a common result is a mixed equilibrium, with cooperation and non-cooperation coexisting in the same population because of frequency-dependency. To see why this would be, let us consider an example.[15]

Suppose some human ancestors live in a context where they can either fight or back down when they come into conflict with another individual over a resource. Let's say that the population starts out full of individuals who always back down. A mutant individual arising who always fights will do incredibly well in such a population, since everyone he meets will instantly back down under his threats, leaving him to enjoy the resource. As a consequence, his fitness is high and his lineage flourishes, at the expense of the nice folk. However, as his descendants become more and more prevalent in the population, they will begin to meet each other more and more often in conflict situations. Every time that happens, a horrible fight ensues which can be costly and injurious to both parties. Once 95 per cent of the population is of the aggressive type, almost all conflicts have this outcome. At this point, the nice folk start to do well again. They don't ever win any contested resources, of course, but at least they don't suffer the terrible costs of all that fighting. Their fitness becomes high, and they start to spread, but as they do so, of course, they make it relatively more advantageous to be aggressive once again. The only possible result of such a situation is a population where the frequencies of nice and aggressive folk oscillate around some equilibrium ratio determined by the precise costs of fighting and benefits of the resources.

Very similar reasoning can apply to the equilibrium level of other-regarding preference. In fact, Linda Mealey and others have suggested a frequency-dependent scenario for the evolution of psychopathy. A rare psychopath in a basically other-regarding population will do well, since most of the individuals he meets will be nice and other-regarding. He will be able to manipulate them to his advantage and further his ends. However, as psychopathy increases its prevalence, more and more of the people he meets will either be psychopaths too, or have a history of interacting with psychopaths and thus be on their guard. Psychopaths will thus do less well. Once psychopathy becomes common, it becomes better to be a rare pro-social individual trying to maintain an island of cooperative behaviour than to be adrift in a sea of Hobbesian chaos.[16]

These considerations suggest that being high in Agreeableness should bring benefits in terms of good social-group relationships, and we know that this is true, but also that it would bring costs in terms of some measure of personal success. There is also evidence that this is the case. Maria, as we have seen, is prepared to sacrifice some productivity to retain good relationships with those dear to her. One study examined personality and career success amongst nearly 4,000 business executives, generally in their forties. Agreeableness score was a negative predictor of their income, ascendancy through the company ranks, and closeness to being chief executive. In other words, the less Agreeable the executive, the better they do, or, nice guys finish last. Another study found that although creative potential is most closely related to the personality dimension of Openness that we will meet in the next chapter, actual success in a creative pursuit is better predicted by low Agreeableness. You have to be ruthless and put yourself and your progress first if you want to get on. As Oscar Wilde put it in *De Profundis*: 'Nothing really at any period of my life was ever of the smallest importance to me compared to Art'.[17]

All this leads to the unsettling but familiar observation that our great institutions—corporations, political parties, universities, and so on—are generally led by people with psychopathic tendencies. Anyone who had the ruthlessness to get to that position thereby demonstrates him or herself not to be the kind of person you would want doing the job. Fortunately, this is only a statistical trend and there are some exceptions. There is another implication, which has less often been explored. When asked what they would like in a husband, women across cultures tend to stress the importance of kindness and empathy foremost. However, they also rate social standing and material success fairly high. But there is a conflict between the two. Kindness and empathy mean high Agreeableness, and personal success tends to mean low Agreeableness. Quite how different women manage this two-directional tug I don't know, but it is a real issue. The kind of person who could give you a glittering lifestyle is quite likely not the kind of person you would wish to share such a life with.[18]

You may have noticed a pattern in this chapter. Maria is a woman, whereas David is a man. Dependent personality disorder is largely a female syndrome, whereas psychopathy is largely a male one. One of the most robust sex differences in personality research is the finding that women are higher in Agreeableness than men are. The difference is over half a standard deviation, which means that although there is plenty of overlap between the sexes, the average man scores lower than 70 per cent of women. Women have an advantage on theory of mind tasks too. Moreover, there is evidence that the difference is deep in our biology. When women are given testosterone experimentally, it reduces empathetic behaviour.[19]

Where might this difference come from? Its existence suggests that, over evolutionary time, women have obtained more benefit from harmonious group membership relative to personal status gain than men. Or, looked at the other way around, men have received a greater pay-off than women from an additional unit of personal status relative to an additional unit of good relationships. There are plenty of reasons why this might be the case.

For a start, the variation in male reproductive success is greater than the variation in female reproductive success. A very high-status man can father a great number of children, the prolific Emperor Moulay Ismail of Morocco, for example, being rather implausibly credited with 888. A woman by contrast is limited in her potential reproductive output to the number of babies she can bear. For men, then, the pay-off of an extra unit of status could be an order of magnitude more offspring, whereas women soon hit a biological ceiling. The benefits of status gain for ancestral men could therefore be high enough to offset a cost to relationships, whereas the balance between the two would have been different for women.

A second and related point is that women often have dependent offspring with them. Human children take an awfully long time to grow to adulthood, and in the ancestral environment, much of the variation in female reproductive success would be variation in ability to keep children alive from birth to adulthood. A woman who was socially skilled would be better able to maintain a network of relationships to protect herself and her children. These include relationships with men, and, perhaps more importantly, relationships with other women. Female solidarity in childcare and subsistence is a notable feature of many cultures. Women are friendship-tenders and kin-keepers to a greater extent than men are. The psychologist Shelley

Taylor has even argued that right across the mammals, the 'fight-or-flight' response to threats is only really typical of males. The female response to threat is better described as 'tend-and-befriend'.[20]

The sex difference in Agreeableness puts the debate about sex discrimination in society into an interesting light. The media tends to decry the fact that the prevalence of women chief executives of large corporations is very much lower than 50 per cent. But is this really evidence that discrimination is operating? It could equally well be the case that there is no discrimination, but that fewer women want to emphasize status gain at the expense of social connectedness. Given the known relationships between Agreeableness and career success, and the known sex differences in Agreeableness, you could actually work out the expected number of women in top positions if the market is blind to sex. It would not be zero, but it would be not be 50 per cent either.

This is not an anti-feminist point, at all. One of the key goals of feminism has been equity. That is, a man or a woman with the same set of aptitudes and motivations should have an equal chance of succeeding. We can endorse this without reservation. However, this does not mean that men and women on average actually have the same motivations, so we should not necessarily expect equal sex representation across all sectors of society. A second goal of feminism has been to celebrate and validate women's values, which are often different from those of men. It is surely more important to value the pro-social orientation many women—like Maria—possess, than it is to lament that they are not more like men.

7

Poets

We have now reached the fifth and final big personality dimension. This is—perhaps fittingly, as we shall see—the most mysterious and difficult to pin down of the five. It is the dimension called variously 'Culture', 'Intellect', or, the label I prefer, 'Openness to experience'. Early conceptions of the fifth factor had it running from 'boorish' at one extreme to 'cultured' or 'sophisticated' at the other. Clearly, culture and sophistication are partly the products of socioeconomic opportunity rather than temperament, and, as five-factor authorities Robert McCrae and Paul Costa wryly note, 'if this characterization had been confirmed by subsequent research, the topic of Openness would perhaps have belonged in a handbook of sociology, not personality psychology'. This may be a slight overstatement of the case, though, since socioeconomic opportunity might lead the horse to water, but can't possibly account for the fact that some people drink more than others. That is, some individuals seek out cultural opportunities against considerable adversity, whilst others for whom they are easily available are not interested in taking them, and Openness could well be what is at work in such cases.[1]

A recent study of leisure activities showed that Openness is a strong predictor of participation in artistic and cultural activities of all kinds. It is not that some people like reading whilst others like going to galleries. Instead, some people are keen on reading *and* galleries *and* theatre *and* music, whilst others are not particularly interested in any of them. This tendency towards greater exploration of all complex recreational practices is uniquely predicted by Openness. (Just two leisure activities were negatively associated with Openness, with the rest all being positively associated. These two were watching soap operas and reading romantic novels. Presumably these relatively low-effort activities are the ones that drop out as the time allocated to other more high-effort pursuits increases.)[2]

Some researchers have seen the fifth factor as 'Intellect', or the propensity to seek out and explore complex cognitive stimuli. At this point, the fifth factor becomes rather similar to the concept of intelligence. Indeed, there are positive correlations between the Openness and IQ scores, of the order of 0.3, which is decently greater than zero. The correlations with the verbal, knowledge-based aspects of intelligence tend to be higher than those with the non-verbal or spatial reasoning components. There are also significant correlations between Openness and years of schooling, which in affluent Western populations is a fairly good index of intellectual ability. One recent study concludes that Openness is a reflection of individual differences in the efficiency of a suite of cognitive circuits in the frontal lobes of the brain. Since the efficiency of such circuits is very relevant to IQ too, this conception places the fifth factor really quite close to intelligence.[3]

However, there are many correlates and constituents of Openness which don't look the same as intelligence at all, but point off in a completely different direction. To understand what these are, we need to explore the one thread in the psychology of Openness that absolutely everyone can agree on, namely, that the exemplar of the high Openness person is the poet or artist. Many studies have shown that Openness is specially associated with flair for, and production of, imaginative and artistic endeavours.[4]

What are poets and artists like, then? It might help to look at some, and where better to begin than Allen Ginsberg's long poem *Howl*, which is an elegy to the artistically inclined young people of his American generation. Ginsberg describes them as:

> angelheaded hipsters burning for the ancient heavenly
>   connection to the starry dynamo in the machinery
>   of the night
>
>   . . .
>
> who passed through universities with radiant cool eyes
>   hallucinating Arkansas and Blake-light tragedy among
>   the scholars of war
> who were expelled from the academies for crazy &
>   publishing obscene odes on the windows of the skull
>
>   . . .
>
> who ate the lamb stew of the imagination or digested the
>   crab at the muddy bottom of the rivers of Bowery
>
>   . . .
>
> who scribbled all night rocking and rolling over lofty
>   incantations which in the yellow morning were
>   stanzas of gibberish

This is a poet writing about other poets and writers, and as such contains considerable sources of insight into Openness. The first thing that is striking about almost all poetry, of course, is its deeply metaphorical content. In the excerpt from *Howl* above, the products of the imagination become a 'lamb stew'. Thus, items from one semantic domain (mental states and processes) interact freely with those from a quite different one (foodstuffs), producing an effect which is arrestingly unusual. It is as if the filters or membranes surrounding different areas of cognition are a little more permeable than normal, and the associations made consequently broader.

A second striking feature of the artistic set described in *Howl* is their challenging of social norms; 'expelled from the academies for crazy'. Though there were particular historical contingencies surrounding the revolt of Ginsberg's generation, the artist as a figure up against convention is a recurrent situation. Ginsberg himself was an active counterculture figure, involved in progressive politics as well as being at odds with the sexual mores of his time. (*Howl* was the subject of a well-publicized obscenity trial in 1957.) As well as unusual social outlooks, many artists seem to have an unusual *turnover* of social outlooks. Ginsberg, like many poets, tried out many different jobs, philosophies, and lifestyles, as well as expressing himself in media as diverse as photography, music, and film, in his continual quest for self-expression. To the outsider, these different periods might look unconnected, fragmented even, but to the poet himself they were no doubt all part of the same journey.

Thirdly, there is a strong sense of spirituality, or even supernatural belief, running through *Howl*. Poets and writers are seen as 'burning for the ancient heavenly connection to the starry dynamo in the machinery of the night'. What is the

'starry dynamo'? Some mystical force, whatever name it is
given, beyond the ordinarily perceptible causes and effects
of physics and psychology. What is the 'ancient connection'
that artists seek? Presumably it is that psychological tran-
scendence of ordinary experience that mystics have sought
to construct since time immemorial. This spiritual quest was
very evident in Ginsberg's own life, with his seeking and ultimately formally endorsing Buddhism as a spiritual system.

Finally, there is a spectre of psychosis running through
Ginsberg's work and life. *Howl* is full of references to hallucination, loss of touch with, or fragility of, reality, mysterious incantations that turn out to be gibberish, and so on.
Ginsberg was writing from experience. His mother Naomi
suffered a psychotic illness in which she heard voices and
believed people were trying to poison her. Ginsberg himself
spent some time in a psychiatric institution, though he wasn't
psychotic and had admitted himself voluntarily. However, he
did have some distinctly unusual experiences. In one episode,
alluded to in *Howl*, he was lying in bed with Blake's *Songs of
Innocence and Songs of Experience* by his side, when he heard
the 'deep, ancient' voice of Blake himself reading the poem
'Ah, sunflower!' aloud. Ginsberg's biographer Barry Miles
takes up the story:

He suddenly had a deep understanding of the meaning of the
poem and realized that *he* was the sunflower. Simultaneous with
the auditory vision came a heightened visual perception: the

afternoon sunlight through the window took on an extraordinary clarity . . . 'My body suddenly felt *light* . . . it was a sudden awakening into a totally deeper real universe than I'd been existing in.' He looked further, into the clouds; they seemed signals of something vaster and more far-reaching than a workman's hand. He caught an understanding of the billions of years that the sea had been evaporating and forming into clouds, each one unique in shape, and of the vast complexity of nature. 'I was sitting in the middle of an entire planetary solar system! . . . I had the impression of the entire universe as poetry filled with light and intelligence and communication and signals. Kind of like my head coming off, letting in the rest of the universe connected to my own brain.'[5]

Many features of this episode are redolent of psychotic disorders such as schizophrenia. Most obviously, there is the auditory hallucination—hearing a voice—itself, but there is also the loss of boundaries around the self, the feeling of special significance in everyday scenes, and the idea of signals being communicated or implanted into his brain by some power. These are all very common in psychotic patients. This incident was not unique in Ginsberg's life, and similar experiences can be found in the biographies of many poets and artists.[6]

The four themes we have found in *Howl* and Ginsberg—namely, broad associations of meaning, restless unconventionality, supernatural beliefs, and psychosis-like experiences—are characteristic not just of poets, but of

Openness as a personality dimension more generally. Moreover, these four themes really having nothing to do with intelligence or IQ, and I will argue subsequently that they point to the more unique and intriguing core of what Openness represents.

Let us take the last theme—psychosis-like experiences— first. There are several reasons for associating such experiences with Openness. First, there are strikingly high rates of mental illness amongst poets and artists, and such people are the very paradigm of high Openness. The illnesses they have are not usually full-blown schizophrenia. Depression is much more common, and, as we have seen, depression is generally more associated with Neuroticism than with Openness. However, the milder illnesses of artists and poets can contain psychosis-like features, and it is not uncommon to find full-blown psychosis amongst their immediate relatives, as was true of Allen Ginsberg. Given the socially impairing and usually chronic nature of clinical schizophrenia, it is not surprising that few people with the full form of that syndrome become eminent in the arts, though schizophrenia patients do very often write poetry or draw, even if it is never recognized. A longitudinal study of the effects of personality through the lifespan found that Openness in early life predicted later involvement in creative activities, but also later contact with psychiatric services.[7]

A second reason for linking Openness to a tendency to psychosis comes from studies of what is known as schizotypy. The idea of schizotypy stems from the observation that, whatever the diagnostic manuals of psychiatry say, the human population does not segment neatly into two groups, those who are psychotic and those who are not. There are people who are considered of sound mind who periodically hear voices, or have some very unusual beliefs about the world. Indeed, many people have the odd experience reminiscent of a delusion or hallucination but nonetheless function perfectly 'normally'. In view of this, it might be useful to put people on a continuum of liability to psychotic experiences. People with diagnoses such as schizophrenia would obviously be up at the top end of this continuum, with everyone else somewhere along its length.

People are assigned schizotypy scores using questionnaires, which are very like personality questionnaires. The difference is that schizotypy questionnaires are constructed using long lists of typical symptoms of disorders related to schizophrenia. People then endorse how many of the symptoms are similar to their own experience. Such questionnaires pass the test of validity in that schizophrenia patients, and even those who will develop schizophrenia in future, score more highly than average. However, the distribution in the general population is a continuum, with some 'normal' individuals scoring really quite highly without obvious signs of life problems. Analysis of these measures shows clearly that schizotypy is not a unitary phenomenon. There are several distinct groups of symptoms, and, whilst psychiatric patients tend to score highly on all of the groups, in the general population you can find people who are high on one group but not the others. Of greatest interest for our purposes here is a group of symptoms that has been given the name 'Unusual Experiences'.[8]

Phenomena that fall within the Unusual Experiences umbrella are hallucination and quasi-hallucination (hearing voices, or your thoughts seeming so loud it is as if they were a voice), perceptual disturbance (everything seeming strange or strangely significant), and magical ideas (supernatural forces, powers coming in and out of the head, feelings of telepathy). Thus, Unusual Experiences is related to the aberrant thoughts and beliefs of schizophrenia, but not to other aspects of that syndrome such as emotional flatness, social withdrawal, or lack of motivation.

When poets and artists are given Unusual Experiences scales, they score more highly than the general population, and, in fact, more or less *as* highly as schizophrenia patients. Where they differ from patients is in the other groups of symptoms relating to emotion and motivation. More pertinently for our purposes here, Openness scores from the big five correlate with measures of Unusual Experiences, with coefficients of around 0.4. There is also a condition known as schizotypal personality disorder, which can be considered in most respects as a mild form of schizophrenia. A number of studies (though the studies are not unanimous on this point) have found that the Openness personality dimension is unusually high in patients with schizotypal personality disorder.[9]

Openness is clearly related to psychosis-like experiences, then. What about our second theme drawn from Ginsberg's life and poetry, namely affinity to spiritual and even supernatural belief? High Openness scorers are not necessarily religious in a conventional sense. They are conventional about few things, and, moreover, tend to be politically liberal and uncomfortable within orthodox institutions. However, high scorers often have strong idiosyncratic beliefs concerning supernatural or spiritual activity in the world. This can take the form of experimentation with exotic religions or creeds, New Age practices, or belief in the paranormal. Openness correlates with a scale of esoteric or paranormal belief with a coefficient of 0.47, which is about the same as the Openness-Unusual Experiences correlation. High Openness scorers also tend to be relatively susceptible to hypnosis, and many esoteric activities have hypnosis-like procedures embedded within them.[10]

The third theme arising from our discussion of Ginsberg was that of norm-defying. It is quite a common finding that artistic individuals also hold—or are prepared to express—beliefs that run against the mores of their time, and they don't seem as governed by taboos on social acceptability as other groups. Is this true of Openness more generally? It seems likely that it is. High Openness scorers are strongly drawn to artistic and investigative professions, and will often eschew traditional institutional structure and progression in order to pursue them. Moreover, high scorers are especially likely to make career shifts from one endeavour to another.[11]

The fourth theme arising from Ginsberg was the expression of broad or metaphorical associations of meaning. I will return to this shortly, as it seems to be a unifying thread, but first, there is a conundrum to solve. We saw that Openness had one set of correlates, namely intelligence test scores (correlation is usually around 0.2). Then we met another, rather different set of correlates, namely Unusual Experiences, paranormal belief, hypnotic suggestibility, and so on (correlation with Openness around 0.4). Each of the elements within this latter set correlates with all the others, as one would hope. However, as a set, they don't correlate with intelligence test scores. In fact, it's worse than that, since Unusual Experiences has been observed to correlate *negatively* with intelligence test scores.[12]

What can be going on? If a personality dimension is a homogenous and reliable construct, then all of the things that correlate significantly with it should also correlate with each other. Indeed, thinking back to Chapter 1, a manifold of characteristics that all correlate together is what a personality trait *is*. So it really doesn't seem right that Openness has two major sets of correlates, which are anticorrelated with each other.

I don't think anyone working on Openness has quite sorted this problem out. It seems to me that there are several approaches that could be taken. One would be to say that Openness is in fact not one personality dimension but two which have been mistakenly lumped together—a trait of quick-wittedness and conceptual dexterity, and then a separate trait of loosened mental associations related to poetry and psychosis. Thus we would have six personality factors, not five. However, this is not the solution I prefer. There is already an extremely well-researched dimension of quick-wittedness and conceptual dexterity. It is called intelligence. Intelligence is not really a personality trait in the same sense that the rest of the big five are. My reason for saying so is that intelligence, in so far as we understand it, is about the global processing efficiency of *all* brain systems. People high in intelligence are good on verbal problems and on non-verbal problems, and on manual dexterity, and even on how quickly nerve impulses are transmitted along their arms. The big five, by contrast, are not about global efficiency of the whole nervous system, but rather about the relative activity of some specific family of mechanisms, be it reward mechanisms for

Extraversion, threat detectors for Neuroticism, or empathy mechanisms for Agreeableness.

My solution, then, would be to say that the 'real' personality trait of Openness is the loosened associations/Unusual Experiences family of characteristics, and that our current questionnaire measures are 'polluted' by items that also tap intelligence. Many Openness questionnaires use items like 'I have a rich vocabulary'. Now, if the respondent takes this to be a question about vocabulary *size*, then the answers will reflect intelligence and perhaps education. If the respondent takes the question to be specifically about the *richness*, that is do I use the words I have at my disposal in unusual or arresting ways, then it will reflect what I am suggesting is 'real' Openness. Similarly, you find items like 'I can grasp complex ideas' on Openness scales. If the question was 'I can grasp how nuclear chain-reactions work', then surely this item would mainly tap intelligence (at least, self-reported intelligence). If on the other hand the question was 'I can grasp esoteric ideas', then the answer would be very different. We all know people who have a fearsome intellect in terms of problem-solving, but are not interested in ideas that are speculative, impractical, or, God forbid, mystical. In my terms, such people would be high in intelligence but low in Openness.

The distinction between intelligence and 'real' Openness is useful for another reason. Openness has often been described as predicting 'creativity', but the paradigm of creativity in such discussions is always taken to be artistic creation, which is a somewhat unbalanced view to say the least. If creativity is the production of objects or representations that are novel and attract attention, then scientific, engineering, and mathematical innovations are equally worthy of the title. However, the psychology of scientific and technological innovators really does look somewhat different from that of artists. The research findings of elevated Unusual Experiences and mental illness rates in 'creative' groups are actually limited to the arts. It is tempting therefore to conclude that artistic creativity is driven by high Openness and all that that entails, whilst scientific or technological creativity is driven by high intelligence. This would be a simplification, since being a successful creative writer certainly requires intelligence, and making a paradigm-changing contribution to science certainly requires some remote imaginative leaps. It might be better to say that the balance of Openness and intelligence required to make a great contribution differs across different endeavours, with an emphasis on Openness in poetry and visual art, and an emphasis on raw intelligence in, say, mathematics and engineering.

I promised to return to the question of broadened associations, and so I shall, for this seems to be the core of what I have characterized as 'real' Openness. It has been known for some time that there are substantial correlations between Openness and performance on 'divergent thinking' problems. An example of such a problem is finding a linking word between three apparently unconnected nouns, such as WIDOW-BITE-MONKEY (answer in the notes). Another is the unusual uses task, where the respondent has to generate as many uses as they can for an everyday object. Conventional uses soon running out, the participant has to seek ever more unlikely juxtapositions: for example, a use for a pair of glasses is to take out the lens and fill it with seed to feed a parakeet, or a use for a brick is as a coffin at a mock funeral for a Barbie doll. High-Openness scorers generate more uses than low scorers, and in particular, the uses they generate are more unusual. This is significant because divergent thinking tasks are amongst the very few classes of test that schizophrenia patients do better on than ordinary volunteers do.[13]

The divergent thinking tasks point to an availability of a range of mental associations to an object which is broader in high- than in low-Openness scorers. How might this work? When an object or the word representing it is held in mind, a lot of related concepts are also partially activated. For example, reading the word SHARK makes it easier to read subsequent words such as SEA and FISH. (We know this from subsequent reaction times.) This is called spreading activation. Concepts are stored in the brain in loose networks of related meaning, and activating one node of the network spreads some activity to adjacent parts. This is probably efficient, since one may well need to move from thinking about the properties of sharks to thinking about the properties of the sea in solving some particular problem. The question is, though, how broadly should activity spread? Should SHARK activate CARTILEDGE, since that is what the skeleton of that marine killer is made of? Should it activate LION, via the idea of top hunting predator in its environment? And what about SOUP, via fins?

There is no right answer to this question, but it is a sensible suggestion that there might be individual differences in how widely activation spreads in networks of meaning. Moreover, the breadth of spread might plausibly be the cognitive mechanism underlying Openness. There is no direct evidence on this question, but there is an interesting study by Christine Mohr on Unusual Experiences-type schizotypy, and as I have said, I see 'real' Openness as quite close to this construct.

In Mohr's experiment, participants saw pairs or triads of words, such as 'HONEY-BREAD' or 'LADDER-BOTTLE-CAT', and had to rate how close in meaning they felt the different words to be. Scores on the schizotypy measure were a good predictor of how close on average the words were judged to be. The higher the schizotypy score, the closer the meanings seemed. The best explanation for these results is that, for the high-Unusual Experiences scorer, each word activates a broad raft of related associations, and since the second word is either in that raft or related to a word which is, the words seem close in meaning. For the low scorer, the raft of associations is narrower, and so the distance to the second word seems greater on average.[14]

If generalized, this effect has a great deal of power to explain what happens not just in schizotypy but in Openness. If every idea or percept generates a broad raft of associations, it is easy to see how some unusual beliefs could be arrived at. Associating what are in fact thoughts with auditory sensation leads to hearing voices. Associating random events with thoughts about absent individuals leads to ideas of telepathy or the paranormal. Essentially, different domains and processing streams which in the low-Openness mind would be kept quite separate end up interacting and being perceived as related. Hallucinations, delusions, and paranormal beliefs are all potentially negative effects of this broadening of associations, but it is also a powerful engine of verbal and visual creativity. The very essence of poetry is an arresting and metaphorical use of words in which meanings from different domains are connected, and similar points could be made using non-verbal examples. Loose associations allow not just the discovery of a solution that follows from existing premises, as traditional intelligence does, but the leap to some totally new way of looking at things, that may yield new fruit or catch the attention of others. This generalizes to the way high-Openness individuals are drawn to consume complex, multiple-meaning representations in art and literature, and the way they may adopt unorthodox social positions, and try out different pursuits. Thus, if I had to bet on what the psychological basis of Openness was, I would put my money on the broadening of interaction between networks of processing that in the lower-Openness mind are kept distinct.[15]

Is such a broadening a positive or negative characteristic? As ever, there is no absolute answer. Natural selection has given us minds containing special-purpose information processors that are very good at solving particular types of problems. Some circuits help us predict the movement of objects, others assess the palatability of foods, whilst still others direct our attention to suitable mates. As a general design principle, you would want each of these to go on relatively autonomously from all the others, since interaction between them would tend to cause confusion and errors. Just occasionally, using associations which originate in one domain on material from a different domain will lead to novel, creative solutions, such as using a plant as a tool rather than as a food, or looking at a fox as a potential hunting partner rather than as itself a meal. Such cases will, however, be relatively rare, and we must assume that selection for most of our deep history favoured processing streams that stayed rather distinct from each other.

However, this situation changes somewhat once language has evolved. Our prelinguistic ancestors were reliant on what they knew innately, could work out for themselves, or could imitate from those around them. Once language develops, there is an additional channel of information, namely what is transmitted from individual to individual by linguistic (and perhaps sometimes pictorial or other symbolic) means. Once a certain symbolic rubicon has been crossed, being able to use language and other representations in a deft and attention-grabbing way becomes a highly adaptive trait. Individuals who can use language arrestingly can command the attention of others. They can get their views and perspectives adopted through the quality of their rhetoric. Their verbal abilities may thus become an alternative source of status to those primordial sources, physical threat and influential relatives. Moreover, as Geoffrey Miller argued in his book *The Mating Mind*, verbal creativity also becomes a potent mate-selection trait. In a symbol-using species, you want offspring who can compete in the symbolic domain, and this means choosing a mate adept with symbolic representations. Individuals would thus select mates displaying the quality of their brains through unusually complex verbal and symbolic products.[16]

The use of verbal dexterity as a mate-selection criterion would have tended to drive up general intelligence in the population, as Miller argues, but it could also drive up levels of Openness. Having greater cross-talk between different domains of thought would produce more unusual and thus attention-grabbing verbal juxtapositions, which, *ex hypothesi*, would lead to greater social attention and perhaps more mating opportunities. Thus, social and sexual selection of this kind would tend to pull against the long history of natural selection working to keep different processing streams in the brain entirely distinct.[17]

Is there any evidence in modern societies of this ancestral socially and sexually selected display mechanism? Well, we do pay extraordinary amounts of attention to poets, artists, writers, humourists, and others who can produce rich and arresting symbolic combinations. They are accorded an importance and prestige in public life which is—and I say this as a great lover of the arts—rather out of step with their narrow utilitarian value. No less a literary thinker than John Carey concluded in a recent book that even after decades of literary scholarship, we still can't say what the arts are for. This is in spite of the obvious fact that many people are deeply interested in them. I would argue that they are not *for* anything. (Or rather, they were not originally for anything. Once they exist they can clearly be used for all kinds of purposes.) Rather, we are selected to pay attention to the verbal and symbolic representations circulating around us, and the arts are just the ones amongst those that are best at capturing and holding our attention. Artists, then, are people who, in virtue of broad mental associations, can produce the most arresting and attention-grabbing representations.[18]

This is not just a modern Western phenomenon. Smaller-scale cultures the world over have strong traditions of ritual, song, shamanism, or other kinds of special, counter-intuitive representations of the world. Interestingly, these very often include psychotic-like phenomena such as telepathy, sympathetic magic, or voice-hearing. I would bet that good shamans or similar figures from small-scale cultures would be high in Openness, just as the poets and artists in our society are.

An obvious prediction from Geoffrey Miller's idea that artistic creativity functions as a mate-selection criterion is that individuals creative in these domains should be especially successful in attracting mates. Helen Clegg and I investigated this prediction using questionnaire information from 425 British adults, some of whom were poets or visual artists of varying degrees of professional success. Mating success is a difficult variable to assess, since sheer number of mates is less important than who those mates are, especially for women. However, sheer number was the only variable we were able to quantify, and for men, especially men oriented towards a short-term mating strategy, this may be a reasonably informative measure.

We found that serious artists or poets had reliably greater lifetime numbers of sexual partners than hobbyists or people who did not produce art or poetry. There are a lot of problems with this study, not least that there will be numerous lifestyle differences between the professional artists and the other participants which are not intrinsically related to their poetic or artistic productions. However, this finding triangulates with several other lines of evidence that artistic creativity is viewed as a sexually attractive quality.[19]

Once humans had to compete for status and mates in the symbolic sphere then, there would have been selective pay-offs for increases in the breadth of mental associations. Such change does not come without cost, though. For one thing, as separate processing streams within the brain begin to interact more, each is made less efficient at the narrow task for which it is specialized. This is presumably why there is a weak negative correlation between Unusual Experiences and intelligence, and why high scorers describe themselves as 'easily distracted'. Low-Openness scorers are probably better than high scorers at solving practical or factual problems, even quite hard ones. There is a potential joke there about how many poets it takes to change a light-bulb, but I will not indulge.

More seriously, though, as Openness increases, more and more remote domains end up being associated, potentially leading to increasingly bizarre beliefs. There is a boundary shared between the aesthetic and the mystical; from mysticism it is but a short step to the paranormal; and from the paranormal, a smooth climb to a delusional worldview. Eccentricity and idiosyncrasy meld into schizotypal personality disorder, which in turn melds into schizophrenia. Thus, if increasing Openness has the benefit of increasing the probability of artistic renown, it has the cost of increasing the probability of a psychotic-like disorder.

One might suppose that there would be a point on the Openness continuum where the benefits and costs were ideally balanced, that is, a value high enough to produce some charisma without the risks becoming excessive. Natural selection would then home in on this point, and the human population would eventually stabilize on a uniform Openness level. This has clearly not happened, since there is heritable variation in Openness as there is for the other four factors of personality. Why might this be?

For one thing, the role of Openness and artistic representations in social and sexual success must vary enormously with local social conditions. In certain ecological contexts, survival is the imperative, and people may be attracted to practical, capable types who might help their families get through the next two winters. In such contexts there would be no premium on Openness. If there is no problem getting through the next two winters, then more imaginative and inspirational qualities may come to the fore. It is well known that certain societies at certain times produce great flowerings of artistic activity. What may be going on in these periods is that, for reasons to do with the local environment, mating and status decisions switch to more aesthetic criteria, giving people a stronger incentive to produce and compete in these arenas. During such efflorescences, there may be natural selection for Openness, whereas other periods are selecting it away.

There is another complexity in the relationship between Openness and reproductive success. Though artistic renown is beneficial to it, having a stigmatized delusional condition is clearly detrimental. Thus the selective consequences of high Openness will be very much contingent on which of these two outcomes results. We do not, in truth, know what determines why, of two people with similar personalities, one develops schizotypal personality disorder and the other becomes a celebrated artist. I suspect that other psychological resources, general health, social support, and opportunity all play their part in which way the marble runs down the hill. Small perturbations in its initial course may lead to large differences in where it ends up. The point is, though, that the fitness consequences of high Openness would vary enormously from individual to individual.

The net result of these temporal and individual inconsistencies in the consequences of Openness is that we will never all think the same way. Some of us will always believe things that others find bizarre, improbable, or of no practical use. Artists will always huddle in cliques believing that society doesn't value art highly enough, though in truth it values art quite a lot. On the other hand, there will always be a sizable

Table 4. The Big Five: A Summary

Dimension	Core mechanism	Benefits	Costs
Extraversion	Response to reward (mid-brain dopamine reward systems)	Increased reward pursuit and capture	Physical dangers, family instability
Neuroticism	Response to threat (amygdala and limbic system, serotonin)	Vigilance, striving	Anxiety, depression
Conscientiousness	Response inhibition (dorsolateral prefrontal cortex)	Planning, self-control	Rigidity, lack of spontaneous response
Agreeableness	Regard for others (Theory of mind, empathy component)	Harmonious social relationships	Not putting self first, lost status
Openness	Breadth of mental associations	Artistic sensibility, divergent thought	Unusual beliefs, proneness to psychosis

cadre who don't see the point of ambiguous representations that have no practical value. There is no answer to these debates. They are what come from us all having different personalities.

We have reached the end of our survey of the big five personality dimensions. Each one, we found, had an identifiable core, based on some family of brain mechanisms, and for each one it was plausible to argue that there were costs as well as benefits to increasingly high scores (Table 4). These are the costs and benefits that have shaped the evolutionary history of the dimensions, but they are also the costs and benefits that modern individuals are likely to come up against in negotiating their ways through life, an issue to which we return in the last chapter. First, however, a different issue. Throughout this book, I have stressed the role of genetic variation in determining people's personalities. This is fair enough, since there is evidence for heritable factors for all the big five. However, to say something has a heritable component is not to say that only heredity is important. There are significant non-genetic influences too, and it is to these we now turn.

8

The Other Half

'The child is father to the man'.
How can he be?

Gerald Manley Hopkins

Throughout this book, I have argued that natural selection maintains a range of different genetic variants relevant to personality traits in the human population, and that it does this because there is no 'best-for-all-places-and times' level of these traits. Thus, a big part of what determines the personality you have is which of these genetic variants you happen to be carrying. This view is well backed up by behaviour-genetic studies, which consistently show that personality traits have a heritable component. However, it cannot be all there is to the story. When behaviour geneticists estimate the size of this heritable component, they conclude that it is around 50 per cent. In other words, around half of the variation in personality traits like the big five is associated with variation in genotype. This means, of course, that the other half is not. There is also significant variation not associated with which genotype you have inherited.[1]

This chapter is about the non-genetic half of the variation. The fact that there is substantial non-heritable variation brings into the frame all those other candidate causes of personality differences that you might have thought or read about: early life experiences, illness, parenting, family structure, school life, friends, and so on. Unfortunately, psychologists know much less about how the environment influences a person's personality than is commonly assumed. People often talk as if the environmental effects had been well understood for decades, and the new discovery was that there were genetic effects too. In fact, nothing could be further from the truth. The area of environmental influences on personality is a morass of unsupported or poorly tested ideas, and, ironically, it is behaviour geneticists who have brought the most progress to the field. The irony is that behaviour genetics was founded in order to discover heritable influences on human behaviour. The methods such studies use, however, also allow us to identify non-genetic influences, and say quite a lot about them. We will look at some of their findings shortly.[2]

How the environment influences personality, then, is still a largely unsolved problem. This chapter will do no more than meet some of the candidate factors and look at their *curricula vitae*. Though we may not be able to identify any single front-runner, we can ask all candidates to take three important tests, and discount any that fail one or more. First, any putative influence must be consistent with the behavioural genetic evidence. Second, candidate influences must produce evidence that is not better interpreted with the causality running the other way around, that is to say, personality bringing about differences in the environment an individual experiences rather than vice versa. Third, the influence must have some evolutionary plausibility, a constraint which I will explain later in the chapter.

First, then, a closer look at behaviour genetics. Behavioural genetic methods rely on measuring some quantity (like a personality trait) across a large set of pairs of individuals. The pairs are chosen in such a way as to allow estimation of various kinds of genetic and environmental effects. The classic design contrasts identical (monozygotic) and non-identical (dizygotic) twins. The former are genetically identical, whereas the latter share only 50 per cent of their genetic variants. In both cases, the twins experience the same family environment (both identical and non-identical twins have the same parents and grow up in the same household at the same time). Thus, any difference in correlation between the identical and the non-identical twin types is likely to be due to the extra shared genetic inheritance. Identical twins are, indeed, much more similar in personality than non-identical ones, and this is one of the sources of the 50 per cent heritable statistic.

If this were the only paradigm available to behavioural geneticists, the evidence would be easy to criticize, since identical twins are probably treated more similarly than non-identical twins. However, other study designs serve to tri-angulate the result. For one thing, there are cases of identi-cal twins being reared in different households, due to early adoption. These twins are as similar to each other in per-sonality as those raised together, and non-identical twins raised apart are less similar to each other than identical twins raised apart. Similarly, non-twin children who are adopted into different families resemble their biological siblings in personality, even though they may rarely or never have met them, and they have no greater resemblance in personality to their adoptive siblings, who they grew up with, than they do to randomly chosen strangers. The correlation is essentially zero.

All this is compelling evidence for heredity. However, heredity is clearly not the only influence, since if it were, then the identical twins, who are genetic clones of each other, would have precisely the same personalities. In fact the corre-lations in personality traits, though substantial, are much less than perfect, and thus, behaviour genetics points up the role of non-genetic factors. However, it also gives clues as to the type of non-genetic factors which are at work. To see what these clues are, let us consider the methods in some more detail.

We can tentatively divide the influences on a pair of siblings into three—not two—types. The first is heredity, the genetic variants they both inherit from their parents. The second is their shared family environment. Both grew up on a commune with a mother who was a professional rodeo rider. The third is what is called the non-shared environment; essentially things that happen to one sibling but not the other. One had a near lethal bout of measles when he was two, but the other did not. One was influenced by a passing Buddhist monk, but the other happened to be somewhere else that day.

Identical twins raised together share 100 per cent heritable influence, and all of the shared environmental influences, and none (by definition) of the non-shared environmental influences. Identical twins raised apart share 100 per cent heredity, but none of the shared environment (excepting the nine months they shared *in utero*), and none of the non-shared environment. Thus, the difference between the personality similarity of identical twins raised apart and the personality similarity of identical twins raised together is a direct estimate of the impact of post-birth shared environmental influence. This study has been done, and the size of that influence is zero. You can do the same thing with adoption. Adopted children share 50 per cent of their heritable influences plus none of their shared environmental influences with their biological siblings, whilst sharing no heredity plus 100 per cent of their shared environmental influences with their adoptive siblings. Once again, you can use this to estimate the impact of the shared environment, which comes out at nil. Perhaps the most directly compelling proof is simply that adoptive siblings growing up in the same household are no more alike in terms of personality traits than any two randomly chosen individuals from the same population.[3]

Given that this is the case, then we cannot avoid the following, rather unsettling conclusions. Parental personality cannot have any measurable effect on child personality (except of course via genetics). Parenting style (to the extent it is consistent across all children) cannot have any measurable effect on child personality. Parental diet, smoking, family size, education, philosophy of life, sexual orientation, marital status, divorce, or remarriage cannot have any measurable effect on child personality. If any of these had consistent effects, then unrelated children who grew up in the same household would be more alike in personality than randomly chosen pairs of children, and they are not. In case you find this incredible, a couple of qualifications are in order. First, there is no question that parental behaviour and family context have effects, perhaps lifelong ones, within the matrix of the family. How parents run the family will naturally shape relationships and behaviour between members of that household. The point is that this does not generalize to the adult personality with which the offspring addresses the rest of the world. Second, the studies on which these conclusions are based tend to include a range of households that are probably all fairly functional. A dramatically violent or abusive childhood might leave lasting effects. Thus, what the studies really show is that across a range of normal family-to-family variation, shared family factors have no effect on adult personality.

This is a stunning finding, and it has caused quite a stir. It is probably the most important discovery in psychology in recent decades, not least because it is counter-intuitive and overturns many entrenched beliefs. Out must go all simple notions about how cold mothers or absent fathers or large families or farm living shape our personalities. If any of these family effects were operative, then they would show up in a non-zero influence of the shared environment. But what about the various research findings reported from time to time showing that children of divorced couples are more likely themselves to divorce, that maternal depression is related to offspring depression, that people who are hit as children turn out more violent as adults, and so on? What studies such as these are actually picking up is genetics. People high in Neuroticism are more likely to become depressed and get divorced, and their kids are more likely than average to do these things too, but not because of the kids learning the behaviour in childhood. Rather, the kids have good odds of inheriting the genetic variants that made their parents like that in the first place. Pretty much all evidence of similarities between parents and children, or of parenting behaviour and behaviour in the offspring once grown up, can easily be explained in this way.[4]

I said that simple notions about the influences of family environment on personality must be discarded, and I chose the phrasing carefully. If some role for these influences is to be retained, it must be a much more subtle and variegated one. More specifically, shared family factors, if they are making any difference at all, must have different influences on different children. One child might respond to parental divorce by becoming highly social outside the home, whilst another becomes withdrawn and introverted. These types of effects are known as person-by-environment interactions. Where they are operative, the same event leads to opposite effects in different people.

Person-by-environment interactions are certainly possible, but we have to be careful here. What is it that determines which way a person reacts to the shared event? It could be the person's genotype. A child with two copies of the short form of the serotonin transporter gene might react dramatically to a negative life event in childhood, and this could have knock-on effects for their developing personality, whilst a sibling with a long version of the gene bounces back quickly, and gains in confidence from the experience. In this case, the person-by-environment interaction is really a kind of indirect genetic effect—a way the environment brings out latent genetic differences. Moreover, gene-by-shared-environment interactions couldn't possibly explain how identical twins reared together still end up with different personalities. After all, they have the same genotype *and* the same shared environment.

The alternative is that the way a person reacts to a shared event is determined by some non-heritable parameter. The most obvious candidate is age. A parental crisis might affect a two-year-old very differently from her seven-year-old sibling. However, identical twins are once again the problem case. They are no more similar in personality if they are raised within the same family than if raised in different ones, and if living together they necessarily experience all shared environmental events at exactly the same age. This would appear to exclude big age-by-shared-environment interactions. Indeed, the only person-by-shared-environment interactions that could possibly account for the behavioural genetic data are ones mediated by parameters that are non-heritable and can easily differ across identical twins living together. This means that although general family factors could conceivably be having some kind of influence on personality, it is a pretty elusive possibility. You would have to say that the family environment has an effect, but that effect varies from person to person according to idiosyncratic factors other than the child's pre-existing personality or age, such that its *average* effect is zero. Possible, but hard to distinguish from the effect actually being zero, and not much different from saying that it is all random.

The first test to be passed for any candidate environmental shaper of personality is compatibility with behavioural genetic findings, and we have already seen some runners fall by the wayside. The second test is not being a consequence of personality differences rather than a cause; that is, not being attributable to reversed causality. The main candidate that falls at this fence is differential parental treatment of different children. Parents do treat children differently, by their own admission, by their children's reports, and by independent assessments. Could the child's personality be what it is because of differential treatment by parents? It could. The problem is that the reverse could also be true. Parents could treat their children differently because those children have different personalities. There is a technique called multivariate genetic analysis that allows these possibilities to be tested in family data. What it shows is that differential parental treatment is explained by child genotype rather than being an explainer of child personality.[5]

The third test that any putative environmental influence must pass is evolutionary plausibility. This test requires some

further explanation. We tend to think about the role of
nurture and learning in a rather indiscriminate way, as if, in
that part of our character which was open to environmental
influence, the environment could write anything it liked with
equal facility, and that any common environmental occur-
rence could be a shaper of the outcome. We are making
assumptions of this kind whenever we claim parental divorce
automatically makes divorce more common in the child, or
any similar theory about parent-to-child modelling of behaviour. We need to think more deeply about how environments
actually affect behaviour, and in particular the role of evolved
mechanisms therein.

Consider, for example, a group of related water-flea
species called Daphnia. One of the forms of Daphnia can
occur either with or without a crest on its head and back.
Having a crest is not heritable. Instead it is entirely determined by environmental factors. Having a crest is protective
if there are predators around. However, crests are costly to
grow, and consequently, crested forms mature more slowly
and, where there are no predators, survive less well. A series
of wonderfully satisfying experiments has shown that if you
hatch Daphnia in environments where there are predators,
they grow crests. This makes perfect evolutionary sense.
The crested form is the better one to have where there
are predators, and the worse one where there are not, so
rather than selection building in either crests or no crests, it

devolves to the environment to decide. But which aspect of the environment?[6]

It turns out that there don't even need to be predators present to induce crests. You just need water that has had predators in it, since predatory species excrete chemicals called kairomones, and Daphnia are able to detect these and use them as a cue in determining their growth pattern. They can even discriminate different predatory species, growing larger crests in response to larger predators. Daphnia are environmentally influenced, then, but they don't develop just similarly to whatever form they first come across. Nor do water temperature, light, and other environmental parameters have any effect on crests. Only the specific kairomone cue has an effect, and it can only do so because Daphnia have a genetically specified, evolved mechanism that effectively says 'if environmental cue X is present, develop a form with more Y'. Such a mechanism could only evolve if X was statistically a very good cue that Y would be beneficial. X, in other words, has to be reliably *predictive* that Y is going to be useful through the individual's life.

When we think about environmental influences, then, we need to remember that adult form can only be influenced by environment to the extent that there is an evolved mechanism to map that specific cue to that specific outcome, and there will only be an evolved mechanism where the cue is a good predictor that the form will be useful. Throughout this book I have argued that certain levels of personality traits are good in some environments and not in others. Thus there would be a strong pay-off if selection could produce environmental calibration mechanisms a bit like those of Daphnia, with the form 'if the environment you are going to live in looks like this, develop a personality with more or less of that'. However, if such mechanisms exist, the cues have got to be ones that are actually predictive of the environmental niches that are going to be available to that person as an adult.

Several more candidates fall at this fence. For example, attachment theorists argue that the mother-infant bond forms a kind of relationship template which the developing person then transfers to his or her important relationships later in life. How much adaptive sense would this really make? The quality of your attachment to your mother is very important for your relationship with your mother, which is a very important relationship. But there is no reason to believe that the type of interaction provided within this *one* relationship is going to turn out to be predictive of *all* the interactions you encounter throughout your life. Your mother might be eccentric, or ill, or have heavy commitments other than you. It would make little evolutionary sense to calibrate your whole personality on something so idiosyncratic. This is consistent with the evidence from attachment studies. Children of depressed mothers are unusually subdued in interaction with their mothers. However, this disappears when they are with their nursery teachers, with whom they behave normally. Of course; what they learn from their interactions with their mothers is what their mothers are like, not what the world is like.[7]

So far, then, we have identified tests that any candidate influence must meet. What are the candidates, and how do they fare? In the remainder of the chapter, I will discuss a number of them, starting with one that probably isn't very important and working up towards one that very probably is.

The first candidate is birth order. The idea that where someone falls within the family has a marked effect on how he or she turns out is a recurrent one. There have been a number of positive findings reported, but also a great number of non-associations, leading two authoritative reviewers of the field, who also carried out the biggest of the studies to date and found nothing, to conclude there probably was no real effect. The idea has not died, however. A recent suggestion is that firstborns are high in Conscientiousness but low in Agreeableness, and later-borns especially rebellious and open to experience. Although some studies find evidence for some of these differences, others do not, and a glance between the studies that find them and those that don't is instructive.[8]

By and large, when one person rates both herself and her siblings for personality, she considers any older siblings a bit more conscientious than she is, and any younger ones a bit more rebellious and playful. However, 'conscientious' is rather like 'grown-up', and 'rebellious and playful' is rather like 'childlike'. When the rater looks back at the personalities of her siblings, she will be remembering, for ones before her in the birth order, someone who throughout childhood was older than her. When she looks back at any who are later-born than her, she will be remembering someone who throughout their period of co-residence was younger than her. Thus, that raters find their younger siblings more rebellious and their older ones more conscientious is a staggeringly unimpressive finding. Where it would get interesting is if the other siblings' rating of themselves, or the rating of them by a third party from outside the family, confirmed the greater Conscientiousness of firstborns or the greater Openness of lastborns. When studies are done using such independent sources of ratings, the effects are generally not found. The only one that looks as if it may hold up is the slightly lower Agreeableness of firstborns, and even this is very weak.[9]

Thus, there is no really compelling evidence for the importance of birth order in shaping personality. Some attempts have been made to frame an evolutionary logic for birth-order effects, in terms of younger siblings having to differentiate themselves in order to compete for resources with their older siblings. This might make some sense with respect to birth order predicting interactions within the family, but

makes no real sense in terms of a calibration of personality in general. A child might learn that certain patterns of
behaviour toward siblings and parents stand it in good stead
in terms of getting attention and resources. This would mean
birth order would affect within-family dynamics, which it
does. Personality traits, though, are the ways of reacting that
are stable throughout our entire lives and which generalize
to all contexts, including the majority of contexts in adult life
where neither parents nor siblings are involved. Why would
it make sense to generalize the tricks that you have learned
for coping with the family situation to, say, adult courtship,
or competition with peers for status? Where you happened to
fall in your mother's birth order is just not going to give any
predictive information about the best ways to approach such
life challenges. In fact, it could be positively misleading. You
might be the least physically imposing child in your family,
but still be more physically imposing than 90 per cent of the
unrelated people you are going to meet as an adult. Thus, to
calibrate your levels of aggression by your subordinate status
in the family would be maladaptive.

Birth order, then, looks like contributing very little to the
explanation of environmentally induced personality variation. Given that this was also the conclusion of a major study
back in 1983, we have to ask why people are so resistant
to letting go of the idea. I think the answer is the same as
the reason that studies find apparent birth-order effects when

they allow the personality ratings to be done by siblings. That reason is that when we think about it, we think about our own siblings. When we look back, we remember siblings who were at different ages to us at the time we had our most memorable interactions with them, and who were behaving in the context of family competition for attention. Thus, they seem very different from us in ways dependent on their position in the family. And different they were. It is just that these differences do not map on to differences in the adult personality that they use now, in the non-family context.

The next candidate to be considered is the physiological environment during gestation. It has become increasingly clear in recent years that in many species, maternal condition during pregnancy can have considerable effects on the growth, metabolism, and even behaviour of the offspring right through to adulthood. For example, rats whose mothers were stressed during pregnancy are more anxious than those whose mothers were not. They are less quick to explore a novel or open environment, and more cautious in social behaviour. In other words, they behave as if their environment is more full of dangers than control rats do. This is intriguing, of course, because it looks very like human Neuroticism. What is happening in this system is that the maternal state—presumably via the mechanism of stress hormones—is acting as a 'weather forecast' for the type of environment the pup will be born into. The pup's responses then get adaptively calibrated to the world it is about to face.[10]

For rats, this seems to be a good system, for several reasons. Rats are a prey species, and maternal stress is probably signalling predation risk. (Indeed, the cue used to induce maternal stress in some of these experiments is the presence of a cat.) Given that the pup will live, initially at least, in the same location as the mother, then the predation risk she experiences is a good indicator of the predation risk the pup will experience. Moreover, the density of predators, although it fluctuates over the years, is reasonably stable over a period of a year or two. This is about the lifespan of a wild rat. It would not make any sense to permanently calibrate one's reactions on the basis of maternal environment if the environment was changing so fast that the 'weather forecast' would be out of date by the time one had reached adulthood.

Do similar effects occur with human Neuroticism? There are reports of increases in psychological disorders in the offspring of mothers who went through severe stresses, such as the death of husbands, or periods of famine or war. Whether these effects, if confirmed, are really changing the personalities of the offspring, or simply adversely affecting their physiological condition, such as to increase their risk of medical problems in general, we do not as yet know. Humans are very different from rats. They are much longer lived, and not so heavily affected by predation. Thus, though the idea is appealing, it is not clear that the system would have evolved in the same way.[11]

Maternal stress hormones are not the only parameter that might serve as a 'weather forecast'. If the mother is mal-nourished, or can provide only limited nutritional resources for the growing foetus, this could be an indicator that the environment is going to be one of scarcity. This idea is a plausible one. The kind of hunter-gatherer societies in which our ancestors lived were highly redistributive. Thus, if one person (one's mother) was experiencing food shortage, it is a reasonable bet that food shortage was general. Thus, as long as resource availability tended to be rather self-consistent over several decades, preparing oneself for scarcity on the basis of maternal condition could make sense.

There is some evidence for the effect of maternal nutrition on metabolic development. Babies of low birthweight, or those born during famines, have cardiovascular and metabolic systems adapted to small size and food restriction. This may have worked well in an ancestral context where food scarcity tended to be a stable feature of some environments. However, when such individuals grow up in a modern environment of calorific abundance, they are especially at risk for diabetes, hypertension, and cardiovascular disease. It is not implausible that certain styles of behaviour are also more advantageous where resources are scarce. For example, if competition is intense, it might be better to be a little less trusting and cooperative (predicting lower Agreeableness), or perhaps risky exploratory behaviours can ill be afforded (predicting lower Extraversion). These are just speculations, but the idea of prenatal influences on personality is one that deserves further investigation. It will surely receive it, too, since such effects are one of the hottest topics in developmental biology. There is one puzzle, though. If prenatal environment were very important, we would expect it to show up as a measurable effect of the shared environment in twin studies, since, obviously, the two twins grow in the same womb at the same time. Such effects, as we have seen, are not found. However, identical twins do manage to have different birthweights from each other, so clearly their prenatal histories can differ somewhat despite their cohabitation.[12]

Prenatal effects could explain one intriguing personality finding. Several studies have recently found that personality measures differ by season of birth. In particular, people born in the autumn and winter months in Northern European populations score higher on a scale of novelty-seeking or sensation-seeking as young adults than do those born in the spring and summer. Novelty-seeking or sensation-seeking are scales tapping into the desire to explore and seek rewarding outcomes that probably belong in the Extraversion family. These findings have not been fully explained.[13]

One possibility is that prenatal and/or immediately postnatal conditions vary with season. A study of an historical

Finnish population showed that infant survival was highest for births during the autumn and early winter. Whether for reasons of disease or nutrition, babies gestated through the summer and born after harvest did best. Autumn-born babies in Northern Europe may still, in modern times, be receiving some kind of early cues of good health. If high Extraversion is a best strategy for individuals in good physical condition, this could calibrate those babies towards a more extravert personality. What the cues could be, and how they manage to still be operative in conditions of modern affluence, is as yet unknown.[14]

We now turn to the final category of possible environmental influences to be considered. A very crucial aspect of the way one should respond to the environment is one's own characteristics. This is a more important idea than it sounds. The extent to which one should be neurotic about sources of harm depends in part on how fleet of foot one is, how good one's immune system is, and so on. Whether one should pursue risky rewards depends a lot on whether one is strong and attractive. The former makes one able to cope if things go wrong, whilst the latter is a big determinant of success if the rewards pursued are social or sexual ones. Whether one needs to be very conscientious in working hard at problems depends in part how smart one is; very quick-witted people can probably prepare on the fly. I could multiply examples, but it makes a lot of sense that evolution would have built into us a capacity to modulate our personalities in response to our health, intelligence, size, and attractiveness.

There is some evidence that effects of this kind occur. For a start, more physically symmetrical individuals are higher in Extraversion than less symmetrical ones. Symmetry is a very important developmental parameter. It indicates how much or little one has been knocked about by mutations and environmental stressors during development. Symmetrical individuals tend to be healthier, and are certainly perceived as more attractive, because of this. Given that one's level of Extraversion is the thermostat of the balance of reward and risk, it would make sense to tweak it to the reward side if one was in great shape health-wise and was found attractive by other people. For men, Extraversion also increases with overall size, though this is not the case for women. This makes sense too, since perceived attractiveness and desirability increase with height for men, but not necessarily for women. Larger men also seem to be slightly less nice, on average, and men with antisocial personality disorder are rather large overall. This is probably because large men have a much greater chance of getting away with the kind of persistent rule-breaking and confrontation that this disorder entails than more diminutive individuals have.[15]

A recent study by three economists shed some light on the sequence in which these influences operate. They found, in two large data sets, a positive relationship between height and men's incomes. Increasing income is a classic sequel of Extraversion, since extraverts are ambitious and competitive as well as outgoing. The data sets provided measurement of height at several points in the lifespan. It turned out that the variable which made the difference for *adult* income was *teenage* height. It seemed that men who were relatively tall at the formative age of 16 became outgoing and athletic youngsters, and this permanently calibrated them to be go-getters. If they became tall by a late growth spurt after this point, it made no difference.[16]

The sharp-eyed reader may be saying at this point, 'this all makes sense, but to the extent that height, attractiveness, and so on are heritable characteristics, then the kind of determinants being described here belong in the heritable 50 per cent of the variation, not the environmental 50 per cent'. This is partly true. To the extent that identical twins resemble each other in height for genetic reasons, they will resemble each other too in height-calibrated Extraversion. In fact, a major way that personality is inherited is probably via genetic variants for stature or health, with consequent personality calibration, rather than by genetic variants that affect personality mechanisms *per se*. However, height, attractiveness, and other bodily characteristics are not perfectly heritable. They are also influenced by sporadic environmental events such as childhood diseases or accidents. The developing personality will calibrate to the consequences of these non-shared, environmental contingencies just as much as it will to heritable variation. Thus, essentially unpredictable childhood misadventures can have important long-term effects on personality into adulthood.

This chapter has examined some of the environmental factors that may influence personality. There are probably others. For example, the niche the developing person is able to occupy in their peer group will subtly affect the way their temperamental mechanisms get fine-tuned. Whether we are talking about genetic, prenatal environmental, or postnatal environmental influences, though, they have all done their work, automatically, implacably, and certainly with no reference to our wishes, long before we have become self-aware adults. This leads us to the question for our final chapter. Can we change our personalities, or are we just stuck with them?[17]

9

Singing with Your Own Voice

There is darkness and there is light. Remember, living is an art.

Henrik Ibsen, *Brand*

The evidence I have presented in this book points to some very clear conclusions. There are (at least) five broad personality dimensions along which we all differ, and which cause us to behave in certain ways rather than other ways. A great deal of what happens in our interests, careers, relationships, romantic lives, and health follows from where we fall along these continua. The determinant of where we fall is how our brains are wired up, and the determinants of how the relevant parts of our brains get wired up are firstly genetics, and secondly, various early life influences over which we have no control and which seem essentially irreversible. This naturally leads to some difficult questions. Does this mean that personality is unchangeable? Is there any more point in striving for personal growth than there is for an adult to strive to be taller? And what about the issue of responsibility? What prevents an aggressive person claiming 'It wasn't me, it was my low Agreeableness, which is largely hereditary'? This final chapter takes a look at these issues. First, though, I must address the question which actually turns out to be the key to all the others. Am I really saying that it takes just five scores to encapsulate everything about who a person is?

If we accept the five-factor framework too naïvely, it certainly looks that way. These five constructs do seem to capture most of the broadly predictable person-to-person variation in human behaviour, and, taken together with intelligence, they constitute the best statistical predictors of life outcomes that we have. But how far should this be taken? Am I really saying that another person with the same five-factor scores as me and with the same level of intelligence would be *identical to me*? This seems an extraordinary idea. Of course, the five-factor framework allows for a great number of different personality configurations—technically an infinite number, since the scales are continuous. Let's say though for the sake of argument that we can measure with sufficient precision to identify ten distinct points along each of the five scales. Since the scales are largely independent of each other, that would mean that there were 10^5 or 100,000 possible personalities. That's a lot of possibilities, but it would still lead to the conclusion that there are about 200 other men in Great Britain with the same personality as me. Am I supposed to believe that they have identical lives to me? Are they all, in fact, also working on books about the five-factor model of personality?

Of course this is not the case. Those 200 men will have statistically more similar lives and relationships to mine than a random sample of British men would have, but they will not be the same as me. We can be a bit more specific about how this works, following a scheme discussed by psychologist Dan McAdams. When thinking about how individuals function, he distinguishes three different levels of specificity. The first tier is the big five personality-trait scores. These, as we have seen, are largely fixed by early biological mechanisms, and they give only rather broad predictive power. At the second level, we can identify *characteristic behaviour patterns*. These do follow from the big five personality traits, but not in a one-to-one mapping. For example, one high-Extraversion scorer might become a polar explorer. Another might take up sky-diving. A third never had the opportunity to try any of these things, but has developed a lively persona in social contexts. The point is that there are many possible behavioural outlets for Extraversion, and which one you adopt will depend upon individual history, chance, and choice. The odds are, though, that if you are a high-Extraversion scorer, you will adopt at least one of them. Thus the 200 other

Daniel Nettle personalities out there in Britain will with overwhelming likelihood have found different characteristic behaviour patterns to be the outlets for their dispositions than I have. They probably spend their time doing things that I can see the appeal of, but in many cases have never done or even considered.[1]

The third level is the most idiosyncratic of all, namely the *personal life story*. This is not the objective events of the life, which belong to level two, but rather the subjective story the person tells themselves about who they are, what they are doing, and why they are doing it. Humans are undeniably narrative creatures. Constructing a personal story is something that we all do, and in all cases, the stories go beyond mere objective behaviours into interpretations, purposes, significances, values, and goals. Once again there is a one-to-many mapping. The very same objective events could be construed as belonging to myriad different narratives. Someone who never achieved much career-wise but had a great variety of experiences could tell their story as one of failure and flaw, or alternatively as one of an enjoyable escape from the rat race. Someone who never married could tell that as either a tragedy or a comedy, depending on how they decided to look at it. The other Daniel Nettles, even if they have done similar things to me, will each have constructed a unique way of narrating the things that they have done, and this unique narrative will have a considerable effect on their identity.

Armed with this tripartite classification, we can revisit questions about the possibility of change. The first level, dispositional traits, does not change very much, in the sense that the most extraverted teenagers are the most extraverted adults. However, whilst the rank order between individuals is largely preserved, the whole distribution undergoes some modest changes with age. As adulthood progresses, people become slightly higher in Agreeableness and Conscientiousness, and slightly lower in Extraversion, Openness, and Neuroticism. This makes a lot of sense in terms of life history. Extraversion and Openness have something in common in that the behaviours associated with high levels of these traits—ambition, creativity, exploration, competitiveness—cause individuals to gain social status and capture resources. As psychologist John Digman pointed out, they serve the functions of *agency*, basically making something of oneself in the world. High levels of Agreeableness and Conscientiousness enhance our connectedness to others, the former by making our interpersonal dealings harmonious, and the latter by making us abide by norms and rules. These are the traits of *communion*, of being a good citizen. Presumably for our ancestors, as now, early life was when status and mating competition was at its highest, and so the motivations of agency were at their most useful. As life progresses, and reproductive success is best maximized by parental and grandparental effort, the needs of communion become greater. Thus, an inbuilt shift in the balance of Extra-version and Openness to Agreeableness and Conscientious-ness makes perfect sense.[2]

Once we move to the second level of personality, namely characteristic behaviour patterns, much more change is possible. For example, a high-Extraversion scorer who rides around on a motorcycle can rationally decide that it is just too dangerous, and take up some other exciting but slightly less hazardous pursuit instead. For every personality characteristic, the set of possible behavioural expressions is very large. People's basic dispositions will surface in some way or other, but they have considerable capacity to decide just which way they will allow it to surface. Thus, if your personality is causing you trouble and worry, you need to find alternative, and less destructive, outlets for the same characteristics. You don't have to change yourself. You just have to change your self's outlet.

Behavioural expressions can run 'against the spin' as well as 'with the spin'. The terminology comes from the game of cricket, where the ball is often delivered spinning sharply in one direction or the other. This gives a batsman two choices. Let us say that the ball is spinning from the batsman's right towards the left. He can sweep his bat from right towards left, too, so that it takes the existing, spinning momentum of the ball and helps it on in the direction that it is already going. This has the advantage of capitalizing on the ball's existing force and trajectory. He can also decide to hit against the spin. This means bringing his bat from the left of the ball, and applying an opposite and superior force to its natural trajectory, sending it back the way it has come.

Behavioural expressions of personality can be like this, too. Those in alcoholic recovery programmes don't limit their drinking to a couple of glasses. They abstain completely. This is just as much of a reflection of their low Conscientiousness as their previous uncontrolled drinking was. They know that if they start, their personality will not allow them to stop, and so they do not put themselves in the position of having started. Their initial excessive drinking was a 'with the spin' expression of low Conscientiousness, whereas their complete abstinence is an 'against the spin' expression. Either way, their behaviour reflects their inability to stop themselves having once begun.

Against the spin behaviours are quite widespread. You can choose to avoid certain people who bring out the worst in you. You can keep yourself away from contexts where aspects of your personality that you are unhappy with will surface. You can not allow yourself to go out until you have completed your piano practice. You can deliberately take a job where you have to see people because you know that otherwise you wouldn't. Changing the way you are by changing behaviour patterns is not easy. It requires using the brain's conscious, executive functions to override or even countermand very powerful, deep, often subconscious mechanisms and urges. It is deliberate, effortful, and has no guarantee of success. Some behaviour patterns are easy to change or avoid, whilst others are difficult to do anything about. Nonetheless, between choosing amongst alternative 'with the spin' expressions of our dispositions, and deliberately creating 'against the spin' expressions, we have a degree of personal latitude in fashioning who we are and how we will be.

We have even more latitude in fashioning how we see ourselves. This is because the third level, the subjective life story, is only rather weakly constrained by temperamental factors or indeed by objective facts. If you have little money, whether you see this as a failing or a virtue is to a significant extent up to you. You can construe its meaning in many different ways. Thus, where it is difficult to change something objectively, you can at least change the way you think about it.

Such reframing is very important in psychotherapy and personal growth, of course, though it is not always straightforward. In particular, high Neuroticism is a constraint here. People high in this trait tend to have quite a lot of bad things happen to them, but more importantly, they struggle to tell positive stories about themselves, even when their life contains much that is objectively positive. It often takes years of hard work, and supports such as cognitive behaviour therapy, for them to overcome their negative comparisons and self-image. Thus, cruelly, those most in need of telling a good story about themselves are least able to do it, whereas those least in need do it anyway.

Our discussion so far provides a useful set of steps to work through if you are dissatisfied with yourself and how you are. As a first step, could you just tell a different story about what you have achieved? If you are the black sheep of the family, who has never settled to anything for very long, you might compare yourself unfavourably to your siblings. But why? Why not think of this as having triumphed in having a rich and spontaneous life, holding on to youthful values, rather than selling out to convention? We all carry useless and outdated notions of what we should be and why, and from time to time these can be shed. Reframing the story, then, is step number one.

Reframing the story might not be enough, though. Some behavioural expressions really are bad, for moral or legal or financial reasons. What if your low Conscientiousness means that you have frittered money away, perhaps through gambling, been in prison, or lost a relationship that was dear to you? Reframing this as a learning experience is a bit trite. You need to change your behaviour. The next step might be to ask whether there are alternative 'with the spin' expressions of your low Conscientiousness to those ones you have been following, and which are more benign. Is there not a job that requires spontaneity and the ability to react dynamically to what is going on? Is there a voluntary activity involving thinking on your feet that you could do to use up your time and energy more usefully? You might need to couple this with 'against the spin' expressions of your low Conscientiousness, too, such as forcing yourself to follow a set routine each morning, or forbidding yourself to go to certain places where trouble can ensue.

If there are readers of this book who feel dissatisfied with their personality functioning, I suspect the most common reason will be high levels of Neuroticism. This is because high Neuroticism infuses everything with suffering. Other extremes of personality—low Agreeableness, for example—have very strong objective effects on life, but people low in Neuroticism just shrug them off. They don't care or worry about them in the way that people high in Neuroticism do. Of course, this is a consequence of what Neuroticism is, namely accessibility of negative emotions, and before you wish it away, you should pause to consider its virtues, as I did at the end of Chapter 4. However, it is beyond doubt that Neuroticism causes awful, private, lifelong pain, hidden away behind curtains and doors, for millions of people. This is a clear case where it is necessary to develop 'against the spin' management strategies, rather than just succumbing to negative emotions.

Fortunately, such strategies exist, and they are really pretty effective. They range from exercise, yoga, and meditation, through cognitive behaviour therapy, to antidepressant and anti-anxiety medications. They vary in how they work. Exercise provides distraction and physical release. Meditation makes the practitioner mindful and accepting of negative thoughts they might have, whereas cognitive behavioural therapy challenges them head on using reason. Medications provide biochemical support to the serotonin system. These strategies do not reduce Neuroticism, but they do allow the person to deal more effectively with some of the problems it throws up. Different things work for different people, but there should be no shame or stigma in seriously exploring all these options and others. You owe it to yourself.[3]

We have, then, very considerable wiggle room if we find ourselves wanting to be different from how we have been heretofore. We also have considerable responsibility. Whilst no-one can hold me responsible for the dispositional traits that I have, since those are not of my choosing, I am morally and legally responsible for the behaviour patterns I develop as an expression of those traits. There are morally good, morally neutral, and morally bad behavioural expressions of all traits, and I am responsible for cultivating ones that are at least morally neutral.

The positive message of this book is that there is no reason to wish one's basic personality dispositions to be anything other than what they are. I have argued throughout that any level of any of the big five is advantageous in some ways whilst being disadvantageous in others. Thus, there is no intrinsically better or worse personality profile to have (and this includes being 'in the middle' for all of them, which has no special virtue in my view). It is rather a question of finding fruitful expressions of the profile we happen to have inherited by capitalizing on the strengths and minimizing the effects of the weaknesses. Viewed in this way, the dispositions you have are a resource to be drawn on, not a curse to be wished away. Let me illustrate this idea with a few examples.

Imagine that you have come to the conclusion, on moral and intellectual grounds, that raising awareness about global warming is the most important thing to which you could devote your time. The trouble is that you are low in Extraversion and high in Neuroticism. This means that you don't come across well on the public platform or in the media. The campaign needs charismatic leaders and speakers who can capture the public's imagination, and when you try to do this, you don't perform well. You feel dissatisfied. Do you give up and do something else? How do you square what your values are telling you with the personality you have?

Bear in mind that the global warming campaign, like any complex modern endeavour, has many facets. As well as charismatic faces, it needs a research effort from people working behind the scenes collating and critically assessing the latest scientific research on climate change. Here you have an edge. The very introversion you cursed means you are quite happy spending a day quietly sifting evidence in the library. The very Neuroticism that makes you nervous in front of a crowd is ideal for worrying away at statistical and methodological details of the studies. The public faces of the campaign will all be hopeless at these crucial tasks precisely because of the high Extraversion and low Neuroticism which you were tempted to envy in them. So, this is the niche you should work to fill. Don't waste your time and energy on the stuff that isn't for you. If you are in the right niche, the rest of the people in the campaign will come to need and value you as much as you value them.

Let us take a second example. It might be that personal experience has brought you to feel that you would like to do something to help young people. So many of them suffer from depression and the urge to self-harm these days. You would like to do something about it. The problem is that you are low in Agreeableness. Volunteer or professional counselling really would not be the thing for you. You would find it tedious and annoying, even though rationally you can see that it is useful. But your low Agreeableness can still be used to help young people. It makes you a hard-headed organizer capable of tough decisions. Those volunteer projects and young people's charities are full of well-meaning but ineffectual people who don't actually run them rationally. They could do with some people like you to get their costs down and their revenues up. You would probably do the cause more good in the long run by working on the organizational side than you would as a mediocre counsellor. You might not make many friends, but you would achieve what you wanted.

We are all embedded in multiple complex social networks—household, community, and organizational—each of which affords many different specialized niches. Whatever the aims and values that you, as an adult, have come to hold as important, there is a way of living them that is consistent with your personality dispositions, as long as you choose the right niche. If you have been plugging away at something and never felt easy in your skin, it could well be that you haven't been aiming at the niche that *you* are good for, rather than one valued by your family or culture or times. You have to be prepared to stand up to those pressures. Modern affluent societies are remarkable for the diversity of social roles and lifestyles they make available. There is space for thrusting workaholics, and homeworkers, and parents, and gardeners, and clowns, and fund-raisers, and scientists, and befrienders. The list is endless. Previous societies were not able to sustain so many different cadres of people. Now more than ever, then, it should be possible to find a niche where the traits you have actually give you an edge.

On the other hand, there are elephant traps to fall into. There are plenty of niches for addicts, criminals, for people who suffer terribly in isolation whilst the world moves on without them, and above all for people who go right through life going through the motions but never feeling that they quite found out what they were for. We have the freedom, the power, and indeed the responsibility to use our minds to seek out the good niches that are right for us, and to avoid the ones that are bad. It is also a matter of understanding the trade-offs inherent in certain choices. If you are high in Extraversion and Openness, you will have no problem with agency, with putting yourself and your interests forward, but you may thereby neglect communion, the connection with other people. On the other hand, if you are high in Agreeableness, you will do communion-type behaviours without thinking about it; but are you pushing yourself forward as an individual enough? Often in life, we may need 'against the spin' adaptations to look after deliberately the things that our personalities don't look after automatically.

None of this means changing your personality. It means understanding what your personality entails, and using this information to make wise choices. This requires many things, one of which is self-knowledge. If this book has helped you achieve a little more of that precious commodity, then writing it will have been worthwhile.

Appendix

The Newcastle Personality Assessor (NPA)

This brief questionnaire allows you to assess yourself on the big five personality dimensions. There follow some descriptions of behaviours and thoughts. Rate the extent to which they are usually characteristic of you.

	Very uncharacteristic	Moderately uncharacteristic	Neither uncharacteristic nor characteristic	Moderately characteristic	Very characteristic	Score
1. Starting a conversation with a stranger						
2. Making sure others are comfortable and happy						
3. Creating an artwork, piece of writing, or piece of music						
4. Preparing for things well in advance						
5. Feeling blue or depressed						
6. Planning parties or social events						
7. Insulting people						
8. Thinking about philosophical or spiritual questions						

9. Letting things get into a mess				
10. Feeling stressed or worried				
11. Using difficult words				
12. Sympathizing with others' feelings				

Record a score for each of your answers, using the following key:

For all questions other than 7 and 9	For questions 7 and 9
Very uncharacteristic $= 1$	Very uncharacteristic $= 5$
Moderately uncharacteristic $= 2$	Moderately uncharacteristic $= 4$
Neither uncharacteristic nor characteristic $= 3$	Neither uncharacteristic nor characteristic $= 3$
Moderately characteristic $= 4$	Moderately characteristic $= 2$
Very characteristic $= 5$	Very characteristic $= 1$

Now derive your score for each of the big five personality dimensions by summing up your score from the individual questions as shown in the table.

Dimension	To calculate score…	Your score	Interpretation
Extraversion	Q1 + Q6		
Neuroticism	Q5 + Q10		
Conscientiousness	Q4 + Q9		
Agreeableness	Q2 + Q7 + Q12		
Openness	Q3 + Q8 + Q11		

Now interpret your scores, using the following guidelines:

- For Extraversion, Neuroticism, and Conscientiousness, 2, 3, and 4 are low scores, 5 and 6 are low-medium, 7 and 8 are medium-high, and 9 and 10 are high.

- For Agreeableness, across the whole population, 10 or fewer is a low score, 11 and 12 are low-medium, 13 is medium-high, and 14 and 15 are high. However, there is a substantial sex difference in scores. For men, 9 or fewer is a low score compared to other men, 10 and 11 are low-medium, 12 and 13 are medium-high, and 14 and 15 are relatively high. For women, 11 or fewer is a low score compared to other women, 12 and 13 are low-medium, 14 is medium-high, and 15 is relatively high. Sixteen per cent of women and around four per cent of men score a maximum 15.

- For Openness, 8 or fewer is a low score, 9 and 10 are low-medium, 11 and 12 are medium-high, and 13, 14, and 15 are high.

A full description of the construction of this questionnaire and the source of the norms is given in the notes.[1]

Notes

INTRODUCTION

1. Our natural tendency to attribute people's behaviour to their inner characteristics, and not to the accidents of the situation, is rather bizarrely known in psychology as the Fundamental Attribution Error. This is bizarre because there is no real reason to believe that it is an error (see Andrews 2001). Other things being equal, assuming that the way people behave is symptomatic of how they are disposed to behave in other situations is probably a pretty good rule of thumb.
2. 'Each assessor has his own pet units': The quotation is from Allport 1958: 258.
3. The five-factor model as the Christmas tree on which findings are arranged: Costa and McCrae 1993.
4. For a review of research to date in evolutionary psychology, see Buss 2005. For the forays made into personality by evolutionary psychologists thus far, see Buss 1991, Buss & Greiling 1999, MacDonald 1995, Nettle 2006a.

CHAPTER I

1. Galton's 'The Measurement of Character': Galton 1884.
2. Galton's 'The Measurement of Fidget': Galton 1885.
3. For a review of the lexical approach to personality, see John, Angleitner, and Ostendorf 1988.
4. The concept of the trait was clarified by Gordon Allport in his seminal 1937 book *Personality: A Psychological Interpretation*, and has

remained much the same ever since. My presentation of personality psychology in this book is somewhat partial. When I talk about personality psychology, I mean personality *trait* psychology. There are other traditions of research that are more concerned with personality processes and the overall functioning of the person than they are with traits. For a history and review of the different approaches, see the papers in Pervin and John 1999. The non-trait approaches do not concern us here, although it seems clear they can ultimately be unified with some version of trait psychology (on this point, see Mischel and Shoda 1998).

5. A system of discrete 'types' of person is a feature of the Myers-Briggs Type Indicator sometimes used in personality assessment. There is no evidence that the discreteness of these types is real (McCrae and Costa 1989).

6. The data used in this example are reported more fully in Nettle 2005a.

7. Early studies detecting five factors in diverse rating data include Thurstone 1934, Fiske 1949, Tupes and Christal 1961, and Norman 1963. For the emergence of the modern five-factor model, see Digman 1990, John 1990, Goldberg 1990, and Costa & McCrae 1992. There are several researchers who should be credited with developing five-factor theory, including John Digman, Lewis Goldberg, Paul T. Costa and Robert McCrae, Oliver John, and others. However, I view the five-factor theory as a gradually emerging consensus position rather than the work of any one scientist, and my presentation here reflects that.

8. Cattell's work can be found in Cattell 1943, 1965. Summaries of Eysenck's three-factor model are in Eysenck 1967, 1970.

9. Stability of ratings over time: The longitudinal study discussed is Costa, McCrae, and Arenberg 1980. See also McCrae and Costa 2003. On consensus between raters, see Kenrick and Funder 1988.

10. Extraverts talk a lot: Carment, Miles, and Cervin 1965. People high in Neuroticism become more upset when thinking or viewing something unpleasant: Larsen and Ketelaar 1989, Larsen and

Ketelaar 1991, Gross, Sutton, and Ketelaar 1998. People high in Agreeableness pay more attention than others to the mental states of characters: Nettle and Liddle 2007.

11. Kelly and Conley's study of married couples: Kelly and Conley 1987.

12. Personality and longevity among the Termites: Friedman *et al.* 1993, 1995.

13. A version of this circularity critique can be found in Bandura 1999.

14. Studies of brain activity and structure as related to Extraversion, Neuroticism, and Conscientiousness: Canli 2004; Omura, Constable, and Canli 2005, Whittle *et al.* 2006.

15. For reviews of the behaviour genetics of the big five personality dimensions, see Bouchard and Loehlin 2001; Bouchard and McGue 2003.

16. The low-consistency and low-explanatory power critique of personality traits is attributed to a book published in 1968, Walter Mischel's *Personality and Assessment*, which reviewed the empirical basis of the whole field. Mischel's important book is often misrepresented. Whilst his arguments are critical or sceptical of many of the claims of personality-trait psychologists, he never denies that there are consistencies in individuals' behaviour that stem from internal, dispositional factors. For example: 'No one doubts that previous experience and genetic and constitutional characteristics affect behaviour and result in vast individual differences among people ... Indeed probably the most striking and self-evident finding in personality psychology is the fact that different persons respond differently to the same objective stimulus' (Mischel 1968: 8–9).

17. This definition works extremely well for four of the big five but is difficult to apply to Openness, as we shall see. Mischel's recent definition of dispositional personality differences is very similar to this one (see Mischel and Shoda 1998).

18. For a fuller discussion of the way the person influences the situation, see Buss 1987.

19. For heritable effects of the person on the likelihood of getting married, see Johnson *et al.* 2004; divorce, McGue and Lykken 1992.

20. Studies showing that personality predicts life events: Headey and Wearing 1989; Magnus *et al.* 1993. Studies showing that life events have a heritable component, and that this is due to personality: Saudino *et al.* 1997.

21. Studies using diaries or pagers: Diener, Larson and Emmons 1984, Fleeson 2001. All of the big five have life outcome consequences: Soldz and Vaillant 1999.

22. The same reward circuitry responds to beautiful faces as to money, food, and other types of reward: see Aharon *et al.* 2001. In this discussion, I am drawing on Jeffrey Gray's ideas of behavioural approach and behavioural inhibition systems lying behind Extraversion and Neuroticism respectively (see Pickering and Gray 1999). Another example of natural selection building a new mechanism by running a feed from an existing one is psychological pain. The pain of being socially excluded seems to activate the same brain circuits as what is surely the more primitive function of a physical pain: Eisenberger, Lieberman, and Williams 2003.

23. For a very different emphasis, stressing how natural selection makes mechanisms independent from each other, see Tooby and Cosmides 1992. The difference between this position and theirs is not as great as it may appear. I don't deny that specific psychological mechanisms show evidence of domain-specific design. However, it is simply empirical fact that different types of negative emotion and different types of reward-oriented behaviour partly draw on common neural circuitry. Whether selection will allow this situation to persist at equilibrium depends on many things, including the fitness costs (if any) that it causes through inefficiency, and the existence of a route to functional independence along which most steps represent a fitness gain.

CHAPTER 2

1. Information on Darwin's finches throughout this chapter is from Grant 1986.

2. Surveys of the prevalence of genetic variation in humans: Halushka *et al.* 1999; Cargill *et al.* 1999. Variation in some genes that is prevalent and widely dispersed: Cravchik and Goldman 2000.

3. Fisher's fundamental theorem: Fisher 1930.

4. Tooby and Cosmides's views on variation are set out in Tooby and Cosmides 1990 and 1992. On evidence of heritable variation in characteristics being relevant to fitness in humans see Nettle 2002 on height, or Nettle 2005a on Extraversion. A more detailed and heavily referenced version of the argument of this chapter can be found in Nettle 2006a.

5. There are a few quite instructive exceptions to this. There are single-gene polymorphisms which have very limited knock-on effects, such as blood groups. Some species of fish contain distinct male types, usually one that matures slowly and competes to defend a territory, and another that reaches sexual maturity fast, remains small, and attempts to sneak copulations without holding a territory. The latter are gleefully referred to by behavioural biologists as 'sneaky f**kers'. In at least one case, the difference between the two male types is controlled by a single gene (Zimmerer and Kallman 1989). The most likely explanation is that all males share the full suite of mechanisms needed for everything, and the 'switch' gene simply regulates the growing and territory-defending mechanisms, turning them on and off at different times or never. In other words, what looks like a qualitative difference is really a quantitatively different regulatory mechanism embedded in the same basic design. This leads us on to the other glaring exception to the no-typological-differences rule; males and females. Here again, the male and female genome both contain the full set of mechanisms needed for making males or females. The master gene on the Y chromosome merely regulates which of these get expressed and to what level in the developing individual. This is the only way it could be done; otherwise dads would be great for making boys, and mums would be great for making girls, and no heterosexual couples would be any good for making children.

6. Though negative frequency dependent selection is a powerful potential mechanism, direct demonstrations of it at work in nature are as
yet relatively few. It is the mechanism that keeps that ratio of males
to females so close to unity, of course, and in the blue-gill sunfish, it
regulates the proportions of two classes of males. One type of male
is a responsible parental investor. The other type, the 'cuckolder', is a
cad and a bounder. Cuckolders do very well as long as they are rare.
However, when cuckolders are very common in a colony, parental
males actually do better (Gross 1991). I leave the implications for
humans unexplored for now.

7. For a discussion of the numbers of harmful mutations that individuals are likely to be carrying, see Keller and Miller 2006. On fitness
indicators and offspring survival in peacocks, see Petrie 1994 and,
more generally, Jennions, Moller, and Petrie 2001.

8. Attractiveness and physical symmetry as fitness indicator traits:
Rhodes, Simmons, and Peters: 2005. For Miller's arguments about
intelligence: Miller 2000; on intelligence and physical symmetry:
Prokosch, Yeo, and Miller 2005.

9. For reviews of personality dimensions in non-human animals:
Gosling and John 1999; Gosling 2001.

10. Lee Dugatkin's guppy study: Dugatkin 1992. I have changed
Dugatkin's terminology in my description of his experiment.

11. O'Steen's research on guppies from different habitats: O'Steen,
Cullum, and Bennett 2002.

12. Research on great tits by Dingemanse and colleagues: Dingemanse
et al. 2002, 2003, 2004.

CHAPTER 3

1. As with all case studies in this book, some details have been changed
to protect the person's anonymity. The case studies prove nothing
in a scientific sense, since I have selected the individuals and the
quotations to suit the arguments I wish to make. Nonetheless, the

case studies are all wonderfully interesting and usefully illustrative, and I am deeply grateful to all the participants for sharing their stories with me.

2. Jung's use of the terms Extraversion and Introversion: Jung 1921.

3. Social behaviour and Extraversion in students: Asendorpf and Wilpers 1998.

4. Studies showing positive emotional states to be related to Extraversion: Costa and McCrae 1980; Watson and Clark 1997. It is a consistent finding that high Extraversion scorers use more positive emotion terms in their writing: Pennebaker and King 1999. For a good overview of the characterization of positive emotionality as the core of Extraversion, see Watson and Clark 1997.

5. Money as an index of social status: Frank 1999; Nettle 2005b.

6. Positive emotions form a behavioural approach or behavioural facilitation system to enable the capture of rewards: Pickering and Gray 1999; Depue and Collins 1999.

7. Studies showing the independence of positive and negative emotion: Diener and Emmons 1985.

8. Experimental studies of emotional reactivity and Extraversion: Larsen and Ketelaar 1991; Gross, Sutton, and Ketelaar 1998.

9. Brain imaging study of emotional responsiveness and Extraversion: see Canli 2004.

10. Activity of the ventral tegmental area and nucleus accumbens in response to reward in rats: Schultz *et al.* 1992; Depue and Collins 1999. The Kool-Aid fMRI study in humans: Berns *et al.* 2001. Nucleus accumbens responses to Kool-Aid predict preference for risk in a computer game: Montague and Berns 2002. Nucleus accumbens and related areas respond to other types of reward such as money and beautiful faces: Aharon *et al.* 2001; Knutson *et al.* 2001.

11. Brain stimulation reward was also sometimes applied experimentally to humans undergoing brain interventions for psychiatric and neurological conditions. The outcome seems to be very similar, with many patients reporting pleasurable feelings and choosing high

levels of stimulation; see Berns 2005: chapter 5, for a good account. Responses to dopamine-like drugs related to Extraversion: Depue *et al.* 1994.

12. Genetically engineered mice and dopamine experiments: Zhou and Palmiter 1995; Giros *et al.* 1996.

13. The initial studies finding an association between DRD4 length and Extraversion or a related dimension were Ebstein *et al.* 1996 and Benjamin *et al.* 1996. For the most recent review and update on this rapidly developing area, see Ebstein 2006. The study of DRD4 and sexual behaviour is Ben-Zion *et al.* 2006.

14. On the distribution of DRD4 variants in the population, and speculations about their antiquity and history, see Ding *et al.* 2002.

15. Association between Extraversion scores and numbers of sexual partners: Nettle 2005a.

16. On the unsettled personal histories of high Extraversion scorers, see Nettle 2005a. Step-parenting as a risk factor for child abuse: Daly and Wilson 1985. Effects of divorce on child outcomes: Amato and Keith 1991; Rodgers and Pryor 1998. There are issues of interpretation of research on parental divorce and child outcomes. It is difficult to demonstrate that the divorce is causal rather than, for example, being a reflection of familial personality characteristics which also cause problems amongst the children.

17. Extraversion and accidents among bus drivers: see Furnham and Heaven 1999: chapter 7. Extraversion and hospitalization: Nettle 2005a. Optimism and longevity amongst the Termites: Friedman *et al.* 1995.

18. On DRD4 population differences and migration: Chen *et al.* 1999.

CHAPTER 4

1. Neuroticism predicts response to negative mood induction and to distressing film clips: Larsen and Ketelaar 1991; Gross, Sutton, and Ketelaar 1998. Neuroticism and daily hassles: Bolger and Schilling 1991.

2. For accounts of the adaptive functions of sadness, see Nesse 2000; Watson and Andrews 2002.

3. On the 'smoke-detector' or hypersensitive design of negative emotions, see Nesse 2005.

4. On interpretative biases and patterns of cognition in depression and anxiety, see Eysenck 1997; Beck 1976.

5. On the brain regions underlying Neuroticism and negative emotions, see Whittle *et al.* 2006.

6. For information on serotonin and the negative emotions, see Nettle 2005*b*: chapter 5.

7. On the serotonin transporter gene and Neuroticism: Lesch *et al.* 1996; Munafò *et al.* 2003; Ebstein 2006. On the combination of brain imaging and genetics: Hariri *et al.* 2002, 2005.

8. The relationship between depression and Neuroticism: Watson and Clark 1988. On the recurrence of depression and its conceptualization as the effects of a personality trait, see also Nettle 2004*a*.

9. The study of genotype, life events, and depression in a New Zealand cohort: Caspi *et al.* 2003.

10. Neuroticism as a predictor of many different types of psychological disorder: Claridge and Davis 2001; Watson, Gamez, and Simms 2005.

11. First-person pronouns and negative emotions in the writing of high Neuroticism scorers: Pennebaker and King 1999.

12. Borderline personality disorder as high Neuroticism: see Widiger *et al.* 1994. A case study of borderline personality disorders is given by Bruehl 1994. High-Neuroticism scorers like 'an insomniac who cannot find a comfortable position in bed': McCrae and Costa 2003: 229.

13. Neuroticism and health: Matthews *et al.* 2002, Neuroticism and immune function: Morag *et al.* 1999. Neuroticism and job satisfaction: Tokar, Fischer, and Subich 1998. Neuroticism and marital satisfaction: Kelly and Conley 1987.

14. On the utility of negative emotions, see Nesse 1991.

15. Study of Everest climbers: Egan and Stelmack 2003.

16. Low Neuroticism in police work: Costa, McCrae, and Kay 1995. Neuroticism related to aggression and rule breaking: Whittle *et al.* 2006: 513. Low Neuroticism in successful psychopaths: Widiger *et al.* 1994: 45; Harpur, Hart, and Hare 1994. This issue is complex, since a large body of literature suggests that on average there is a small *positive* correlation between Neuroticism and criminality, Cale 2006.

17. Rates of depression in writers and artists: Andreasen 1987; Jamison 1989; Ludwig 1995.

18. Neuroticism and workaholism: Burke, Matthiesen, and Pallesen 2006. Neuroticism and attainment amongst university students: McKenzie, Taghavi-Khonsary, and Tindell 2000.

19. People are over-optimistic and under-reflective: Taylor and Brown 1992; Nettle 2004b. For the military case, see Johnson 2004.

20. Implementational and deliberative mindsets: Taylor and Gollwitzer 1995.

21. Over-optimism in normal subjects and 'depressive realism': Dobson and Franche 1989. Neuroticism and occupational success in professional occupations: Barrick and Mount 1991.

22. See Randolph Nesse, 'Is the market on Prozac?' published at <http://www.edge.org>.

CHAPTER 5

1. The patient who took cars and drove them away: Cohen *et al.* 1999.

2. The Iowa gambling task: Bechara *et al.* 1994.

3. Up to 1 per cent of people meet the criteria for pathological gambling: Phillips 2006. Pathological gamblers and the Iowa gambling task: Cavedini *et al.* 2002.

4. Iowa gambling task in addictions: Bechara *et al.* 2001; Bolla *et al.* 2005.

5. Slutske's study of co-morbidity of problem gambling and substance dependency: Slutske *et al.* 2005.

6. Studies of the co-occurrence of gambling, addictions, and antisocial behaviour: Swendsen *et al.* 2002; Black *et al.* 2006; Livesley *et al.* 1998; Krueger 1999; Slutske *et al.* 2005.

7. Studies of which personality characteristics predict the development of addiction problems: Slutske *et al.* 2005; Swendsen *et al.* 2002. Addicts also have elevated Neuroticism, which is no surprise, since Neuroticism is the index of disturbed psychological functioning of all kinds. However, it is the Conscientiousness differences that uniquely identify those vulnerable to problem gambling and addictions.

8. Addiction as the failure of inhibitory mechanisms rather than the size of reward response: Volkow and Fowler 2000; Lubman, Yücel, and Pantelis 2004.

9. Brain activity associated with impulsivity in tasks like the Iowa: Horn *et al.* 2003; Bolla *et al.* 2005. See also Whittle *et al.* 2006 for a review. I have simplified what is known of frontal lobe functioning here. In addicts, the orbitofrontal cortex, though generally underactive, can become temporarily *overactive* specifically when the participant is craving or is exposed to cues associated with the drug; see Volkow and Fowler 2000.

10. Brain imaging and the Go-No Go task: Asahi *et al.* 2004.

11. Conscientiousness and occupational success: Barrick and Mount 1991.

12. Autonomy mediates the Conscientiousness-occupational success relationship: Barrick and Mount 1993. Goal-setting and execution and Conscientiousness at work: Barrick, Mount, and Strauss 1993.

13. Conscientiousness and intelligence: Moutafi, Furnham, and Paltiel 2005.

14. Attention-deficit hyperactivity disorder and personality: Nigg *et al.* 2002; Retz *et al.* 2004.

15. Obsessive-compulsive personality disorder is extreme Conscientiousness: see Widiger *et al.* 1994. Prevalence of obsessive-compulsive personality disorder: Coid *et al.* 2006. There is a strange fact about Conscientiousness, which is that the average level is the same in men

and women, and yet the disorders of both very low Conscientiousness (gambling, alcoholism, ADHD, antisocial personality disorder)
and very high Conscientiousness (obsessive-compulsive personality
disorder) are more prevalent amongst men, by a factor of about
2 to 1.

16. Obsessive-compulsive disorder similar to low Conscientiousness
conditions like addictions: Lubman, Yücel, and Pantelis 2004.
17. Definition of obsessive-compulsive personality disorder: APA 2000.
The case study of Ronald: Nolen-Hoeksema 2007: 451–2.
18. Relationships of personality and OCPD to anorexia nervosa: Lilenfeld *et al.* 2006.

CHAPTER 6

1. Experiments with chimpanzees: Silk *et al.* 2005; Jensen *et al.* 2006.
2. Chimpanzee theory of mind rudimentary at best: Call 2001. In this
account, I use theory of mind, for convenience, as the superordinate
term covering both mentalizing and empathizing. There is some
variation in usage in the literature, with some authors restricting
theory of mind to non-emotional mentalizing, or not using all these
terms.
3. The Sally-Anne task: Wimmer and Perner 1983.
4. Theory of mind in autism: Baron-Cohen, Leslie, and Frith 1985.
Theory of mind stories task: Kinderman, Dunbar, and Bentall 1998;
Stiller and Dunbar 2007.
5. Theory of mind performance and social networks: Stiller and
Dunbar 2007. Children's version of theory of mind stories task: Liddle and Nettle 2006.
6. Brain-imaging studies of mentalizing and empathizing: Völlm *et al.*
2006.
7. The empathy quotient is highly correlated with Agreeableness:
Nettle 2007. Performance on the theory of mind stories task and
Agreeableness: Nettle and Liddle 2007.

8. Experiment on time spent processing words and Agreeableness: Wilkowski, Robinson and Meier 2006. Characterization of people high in Agreeableness: Asendorpf and Wilpers 1998; Soldz and Vaillant 1999; Penner *et al.* 2005; Meier and Robinson 2004.

9. Relationship of psychopathy to the big five: Harpur, Hart, and Hare 1994; Lynam *et al.* 2005. Psychopathy is not a recognized category in current manuals of psychiatric diagnosis. The closest category is antisocial personality disorder, but this broad syndrome is clearly heterogeneous. Its definition focuses on antisocial behaviour rather than underlying psychological attributes. It has been estimated that 80 per cent of the prison population would qualify for a diagnosis of antisocial personality disorder (Hart and Hare 1996). However, there are many different reasons people might behave in an antisocial manner, psychopathy being only one of them. The term sociopath is sometimes used with a similar meaning to psychopath. The diagnosis of narcissistic personality disorder also captures something of the egocentricity and lack of empathy characteristic of low Agreeableness.

10. Agreeableness, Conscientiousness and Neuroticism as the checks against antisocial behaviour: I am simplifying the role of Neuroticism here. Research tends to suggest that antisocial individuals are either very low in Neuroticism (the classic psychopathic criminal with no fear of consequences), or else higher than average (people who experience so much negative affect that they lash out desperately). The best check against antisociality may thus be an average level of Neuroticism. See Harpur, Hart, and Hare 1994; Lynam *et al.* 2005; Cale 2006.

11. Autism and psychopathy: I am drawing upon Blair *et al.* 1996; Dolan and Fullum 2004; and Völlm *et al.* 2006 here.

12. Agreeableness, the stories task, and the 'reading the mind in the eyes' test: Nettle and Liddle 2007.

13. Ultimate explanations for other-regarding preferences: Fehr and Fischbacher 2003; Penner *et al.* 2005. Gossip and information-sharing linked to human pro-sociality: Dunbar 1996; Nettle 2006*b*.

14. Dependent personality disorder: Widiger *et al.* 1994.
15. Models of the evolution of cooperative behaviour: Maynard-Smith 1982.
16. Frequency-dependent models of psychopathy: Mealey 1995. See also Troisi 2005.
17. Career success and Agreeableness in executives: Boudreau, Boswell, and Judge 2001. Agreeableness and attainment in creative fields: King, Walker, and Broyles 1996. Note that low Agreeableness may be useful for attaining high status, but it is not sufficient. Extraversion—the desire to pursue rewards—is important too. David in this chapter is low in Agreeableness but also very low in Extraversion, which means he has no desire to pursue high status. Oscar Wilde quote: Wilde 1973: 101.
18. On the trade-off between Agreeableness and personal success as it applies to mate choice: Nettle and Clegg 2007.
19. Sex differences in Agreeableness: Costa, Terraciano, and McCrae 2001. See also Nettle 2007. Sex differences on theory of mind task: Stiller and Dunbar 2007. Testosterone administration and empathy in women: Hermans, Putnam, and van Honk 2006.
20. Female mammals having a 'tend-and-befriend' rather than 'fight-or-flight' response: Taylor *et al.* 2000.

CHAPTER 7

1. On the characterization of the Openness dimension, I am drawing on McCrae and Costa 1997. The quote is from page 830.
2. Personality and recreational activities: Kraaykamp and van Eijck 2005.
3. Openness, frontal lobe function, and intelligence: DeYoung, Peterson, and Higgins 2005.
4. Openness and artistic interests: Costa, McCrae, and Holland 1984; McCrae and Costa 1987.
5. Ginsberg's William Blake vision: Miles 1989: 100.

6. Psychosis-like episodes in the lives of poets and artists: See, for example, Claridge, Pryor, and Watkins 1990.

7. On mental illness amongst poets and artists, see Nettle 2001 for a review. Openness predicts later contact with psychiatrists: Soldz and Vaillant 1999.

8. Schizotypy: For a wealth of information about research in this area, see Claridge 1997.

9. Schizotypy in poets and artists: Nettle 2006c; Burch *et al.* 2006*a*. Unusual Experiences correlates with Openness: Rawlings and Freeman 1997; Burch *et al.* 2006*b*. Openness high in schizotypal personality disorder: Gurrera *et al.* 2005.

10. Correlations between Openness and esoteric/paranormal belief, and between Openness and hypnotic suggestibility: McCrae and Costa 1987.

11. Artists break taboos of respectability: Burch *et al.* 2006*a*. Openness predicts career shifts: McCrae and Costa 1987: 841.

12. Negative correlation of intelligence test scores and Unusual Experiences: Burch *et al.* 2006*b*.

13. Answer to WIDOW-BITE-MONKEY: SPIDER. On Openness and divergent thinking tasks: McCrae 1987. Performance of schizophrenia patients on divergent thinking tasks: Keefe and Magaro 1980; see Nettle 2001 for a discussion. Divergent thinking tasks are reasonably independent of general intelligence, on which schizophrenia patients generally have a mild deficit. Intelligence test tasks always converge on a single correct answer, which may be difficult to compute, whereas divergent thinking tasks have an unlimited set of possible responses.

14. Study of semantic similarity and schizotypy: Mohr *et al.* 2001.

15. Openness as broadening of associations: There is also evidence, not discussed here, concerning the role of attention in Openness or Unusual Experiences. In tasks where they have to ignore one set of stimuli in favour of another, high scorers also show evidence of failing to inhibit the information that they are supposed to be ignoring, as evidenced by the later performance on tasks probing reaction to

the ignored stimuli. These attentional phenomena must be some-
how related to broadened associations more generally; see Green
and Williams 1999; Peterson and Carson 2000; Burch, Hemsley, and
Joseph 2004.

16. Miller's idea of creativity as a mate-selection trait: Miller 2000.

17. For an interesting discussion of separateness and fluidity of different
information processes in the mind over evolutionary history, see
Mithen 1999. Mithen sees increased fluidity—increased Openness,
in our terms—as the hallmark of fully modern *Homo sapiens*.

18. John Carey's recent book: Carey 2005.

19. Study of British poets and artists: Nettle and Clegg 2006. Other lines
of evidence that artistic creativity is used in mate selection: Haselton
and Miller 2006.

CHAPTER 8

1. The amount of variation in personality not associated with heredity and which has a non-factitious cause might actually be smaller
than 50 per cent. Personality inventories have a test-retest reliability
of less than 1. This means that there is some day-to-day fluctuation, and so two identical twins with exactly the same personality
who took the same test might have non-identical scores. The variation associated with these vagaries of measurement tends to get
lumped into the estimate of environmental influence, and when
it is controlled for, the magnitude of the environmental influence
goes down (Plomin, Asbury, and Dunn 2001: 228). Moreover, self-
report personality measures probably overestimate the amount of
cross-situation consistency in people's behaviour. When objective
measurements are used instead of self-rating, it looks like genetic
factors can account for the preponderance of cross-situational consistency in behaviour (see Harris 2006: 120). Thus, it would be
mainly heredity determining our consistent behavioural signature
across all situations, and mainly non-shared environment (i.e. our

history of learning) determining the situation-specific components of behaviour. This is an intriguing possibility, but in this chapter I follow the more conventional line that there is a sizable non-shared environmental component in broad personality traits to be explained.

2. How the environment influences personality is still a mystery: see Turkheimer and Waldron 2000 for a review.

3. Behaviour-genetic studies of effect of heredity, non-shared environment, and shared environment on personality: Plomin and Daniels 1987; Bouchard and McGue 2003.

4. The lack of an effect of the shared environment has caused quite a stir: See Plomin and Daniels 1987 (and commentaries therein); Plomin, Asbury, and Dunn 2001, Harris 2006 for some interesting discussions of these findings and reactions to them.

5. Differential parental treatment in multivariate genetic analysis: Plomin, Asbury, and Dunn 2001.

6. Crest development in Daphnia: Grant and Bayly 1981; Barry 1994.

7. Attachment theory: Bowlby 1969. Children of depressed mothers: Pelaez-Nogueras *et al.* 1994; Harris 2006.

8. Authoritative reviewers of the birth order and personality literature: Ernst and Angst 1983. The idea that firstborns are high in Conscientiousness and low in Agreeableness, whilst later-borns are rebellious and high in Openness: Sulloway 1996.

9. Studies that ask people to rate their siblings and get birth-order effects: Paulhus, Trapnell, and Chen 1999; Healey and Ellis 2007. Studies that use self- or independent ratings of personality and find few if any birth-order effects: Ernst and Angst 1983; Jefferson, Herbst, and McCrae 1998; Parker 1998; Beer and Horn 2000; Michalski and Shackleford 2002. A small decrement in Agreeableness in firstborns does show up in some of the reliable studies (Michalski and Shackleford 2002; Jefferson, Herbst, and McCrae 1998). Incidentally, Sulloway's (1996) argument about birth order and personality was not made using standard personality data, but instead from historical and biographical information. Severe doubt has been

cast on the evidential basis of his claims (Townsend 2000; Johnson 2000).

10. Maternal stress and rat behaviour: Patin *et al.* 2005. The idea of a maternal 'weather forecast': Bateson *et al.* 2004.

11. Maternal stress and psychopathology in humans: See Patin *et al.* 2005: 265–6.

12. Prenatal effects is a hot topic in developmental biology: Bateson *et al.* 2004. Paternal effects can occur as well as maternal ones (via biochemical information in sperm), and the effects can actually persist for more than one generation (the grandparent sets the physiology of the parent, who sets the physiology of the offspring): Pembrey *et al.* 2006.

13. Season of birth and personality: Chotai *et al.* 2002, 2003; Joinson and Nettle 2005. Note a non-replication in a US sample: Hartmann, Reuter, and Nyborg 2006.

14. Birth season and survival in historical Finns: Lummaa *et al.* 1998.

15. Extraversion and symmetry: Fink *et al.* 2005; Pound 2006. Large men but not women found more attractive: Nettle 2002. Extraversion and size: Faith *et al.* 2001. Larger men less nice: Faith *et al.* 2001. Size and antisocial personality disorder: Ishikawa *et al.* 2001.

16. Economists study height and men's incomes: Persico, Postlethwaite, and Silverman 2004.

17. For an exploration of peer group influences on personality, see Harris 2006.

CHAPTER 9

1. In this discussion I am drawing on McAdams's (1996, 1999) distinctions between dispositional traits, characteristic adaptations, and integrative life stories. I have changed his terminology for characteristic adaptations to characteristic behavioural patterns since, as an evolutionist, 'adaptation' has a quite specific meaning for me.

2. Digman's communion and agency: Digman 1997. Changes in personality across the lifespan: McCrae and Costa 2003.

3. On anti-Neuroticism strategies, see Nettle 2005b for a discussion. For more practical advice, I recommend Gilbert 1997 (a UK-published book of cognitive-behavioural-therapy-based self-help), and McQuaid and Carmona 2004 (a US book on mindfulness and meditation to combat depression). There are many other good self-help resources available, but beware those whose promises are unrealistic.

APPENDIX

1. The Newcastle Personality Assessor is one of a number of very brief instruments for assessing the big five which have been developed recently (see Gosling, Rentfrow, and Swann 2003; Rammstedt and John 2007). The authors of these instruments have found that even a very small number of carefully chosen items produce scores that correlate quite highly with those derived from the much longer questionnaires which are more traditionally used. Thus, despite the small number of items, the scores given by these brief instruments are quite informative.

The Newcastle Personality Assessor was constructed by administering a pool of 26 candidate items to a large online sample of adults, along with the 50-item five-factor questionnaire from the International Personality Item Pool, and several other scales. The IPIP scale is a well-validated five-factor instrument (see Gow *et al.* 2005, Goldberg *et al.* 2006). Recruitment was via a psychology research website and appeals for volunteers on community fora. There were 563 people in the sample (169 men, 394 women), with a mean age of 34.87 years (standard deviation 13.17, range 16–80). Items were selected for the NPA on the basis of their correlations with the IPIP scores, and in two cases items from the IPIP questionnaire were adopted in modified form into the NPA due to the unsatisfactory performance of my own items. Each personality dimension was represented by either two or three items as required to give a correlation with the IPIP score of above 0.7, and a reasonable spread of scores. The correlations between NPA and IPIP scores for the big five are as follows: Extraversion 0.77, Neuroticism 0.82, Conscientiousness 0.77, Agreeableness 0.77, Openness 0.74. The different items for each dimension all correlate significantly with each other. The norms given are produced by dividing the distribution as nearly as possible into quartiles, so 'low' represents approximately the bottom 25 per cent of the population, 'low-medium' the next 25 per cent, and so on.

You are welcome to copy and use the NPA, but where time permits, a longer instrument such as the IPIP questionnaire (which I favour because it is made so freely available by those who developed it; see <http://ipip.ori.org/ipip/>) is preferable.

References

Aharon, I. *et al.* (2001). Beautiful faces have variable reward value: fMRI and behavioral evidence. *Neuron*, 32: 537–51.

Allport, G. W. (1937). *Personality: A Psychological Interpretation* (New York: Holt).

_____ (1958). What units shall we employ? In G. Lindzey (ed.), *Assessment of Human Motives* (New York: Rinehart), 238–60.

Amato, P. R. and Keith, B. (1991). Parental divorce and the well-being of children: A meta-analysis. *Psychological Bulletin*, 110: 26–46.

Andreasen, N. C. (1987). Creativity and mental illness: Prevalence rates in writers and their first-degree relatives. *American Journal of Psychiatry*, 144: 1288–92.

Andrews, P. (2001). The psychology of social chess and the evolution of attribution mechanisms: Explaining the fundamental attribution error. *Evolution and Human Behavior*, 22: 11–29.

APA (2000). *Diagnostic and Statistical Manual of Mental Disorders. Fourth Edition—Text Revision* (Washington, DC: American Psychiatric Association).

Asahi, S. *et al.* (2004). Negative correlation between right prefrontal activity during response inhibition and impulsiveness: An fMRI study. *European Archives of Psychiatry and Clinical Neuroscience*, 254: 245–51.

Asendorpf, J. B. and Wilpers, S. (1998). Personality effects on social relationships. *Journal of Personality and Social Psychology*, 74: 1531–44.

Bandura, A. (1999). Social cognitive theory of personality. In L. A. Pervin and O. P. John (eds.), *Handbook of Personality Psychology: Theory and Research*, 2nd edn. (New York: Guilford Press), 154–96.

Baron-Cohen, S., Leslie, A., and Frith, U. (1985). Does the autistic child have a theory of mind? *Cognition*, 21: 37–46.

Barrick, M. R. and Mount, M. K. (1991). The big five personality dimensions and job performance: A meta-analysis. *Personnel Psychology*, 44: 1–26.

———— (1993). Autonomy as a moderator of the relationships between the big five personality dimensions and job performance. *Journal of Applied Psychology*, 78: 111–18.

———— and Strauss, J. P. (1993). Conscientiousness and performance of sales representatives: Test of the mediating effects of goal setting. *Journal of Applied Psychology*, 78: 715–22.

Barry, M. J. (1994). The costs of crest induction for *Daphnia carinata*. *Oecologia*, 97: 278–88.

Bateson, P. *et al.* (2004). Developmental plasticity and human health. *Nature*, 430: 419–21.

Bechara, A. *et al.* (1994). Insensitivity to future consequences following damage to human prefrontal cortex. *Cognition*, 50: 7–15.

———— (2001). Decision-making deficits, linked to a dysfunctional ventromedial prefrontal cortex, revealed in alcohol and stimulant abusers. *Neuropsychologia*, 39: 376–89.

Beck, A. T. (1976). *Cognitive Therapy and the Emotional Disorders* (New York: International Universities Press).

Benjamin, J. *et al.* (1996). Population and familial association between the D4 dopamine receptor gene and measures of Novelty Seeking. *Nature Genetics*, 12: 81–4.

Ben-Zion, I. Z. *et al.* (2006). Polymorphisms in the dopamine D4 receptor gene (DRD4) contribute to individual differences in human sexual behavior: Desire, arousal and sexual function. *Molecular Psychiatry*, 11: 782–6.

Beer, J. M. and Horn, J. M. (2000). The influence of rearing order on personality development within two adoption cohorts. *Journal of Personality*, 68: 769–819.

Berns, G. (2005). *Satisfaction: The Science of Finding True Fulfilment* (New York: Henry Holt).

Berns, G. *et al.* (2001). Predictability modulates human brain response to reward. *Journal of Neuroscience*, 21: 2793–8.

Black, D. W. *et al.* (2006). A family study of pathological gambling. *Psychiatry Research*, 141: 295–303.

Blair, J. *et al.* (1996). Theory of mind in the psychopath. *Journal of Forensic Psychiatry*, 7: 15–25.

Bolger, N. and Schilling E. A. (1991). Personality and the problems of everyday life: the role of neuroticism in exposure and reactivity to daily stressors. *Journal of Personality*, 59: 335–86.

Bolla, K. I. *et al.* (2005). Neural substrates of faulty decision-making in abstinent marijuana users. *Neuroimage*, 26: 480–92.

Bouchard, T. J. and Loehlin, J. C. (2001). Genes, evolution, and personality. *Behavior Genetics*, 31: 243–73.

_____ and McGue, M. (2003). Genetic and environmental influences on human psychological differences. *Journal of Neurobiology*, 54: 4–45.

Boudreau, J. W., Boswell, W. R., and Judge, T. A. (2001). Effects of personality on executive career success in the United States and Europe. *Journal of Vocational Behaviour*, 58: 53–81.

Bowlby, J. (1969). *Attachment and Loss. Volume 1: Attachment* (New York: Basic Books).

Bruehl, S. (1994). A case of borderline personality disorder. In P. T. Costa and T. A. Widiger (eds.), *Personality Disorders and the Five-Factor Model of Personality* (Washington, DC: American Psychological Association), 189–98.

Burch, G. St. J., Hemsley, D. R., and Joseph, M. H. (2004). Trials-to-criterion latent inhibition in humans as a function of stimulus pre-exposure and positive schizotypy. *British Journal of Psychology*, 95: 179–96.

_____ *et al.* (2006a). Schizotypy and creativity in visual artists. *British Journal of Psychology*, 97: 177–90.

_____ (2006b). Personality, creativity and latent inhibition. *European Journal of Personality*, 20: 107–22.

Burke, R. J., Matthiesen, S. B., and Pallesen, S. (2006). Personality correlates of workaholism. *Personality and Individual Differences*, 40: 1223–33.

Buss, D. M. (1987). Selection, evocation and manipulation. *Journal of Personality and Social Psychology*, 53: 1214–21.

——— (1991). Evolutionary personality psychology. *Annual Review of Psychology*, 42: 459–91.

——— (ed.) (2005). *Handbook of Evolutionary Psychology*, (New York: Wiley).

——— and Greiling, H. (1999). Adaptive individual differences. *Journal of Personality*, 67: 209–43.

Cale, E. M. (2006). A quantitative review of the relations between the 'Big 3' higher order personality dimensions and antisocial behavior. *Journal of Research in Personality*, 40: 250–84.

Call, J. (2001). Chimpanzee social cognition. *Trends in Cognitive Sciences*, 5: 388–93.

Canli, T. (2004). Functional brain mapping of Extraversion and Neuroticism: Learning from individual differences in emotion processing. *Journal of Personality*, 72: 1105–31.

Carey, J. (2005). *What Good are the Arts?* (London: Faber & Faber).

Cargill, M. *et al.* (1999). Characterization of single-nucleotide polymorphisms in coding regions of human genes. *Nature Genetics*, 22: 231–8.

Carment, D. W., Miles, C. G., and Cervin, V. B. (1965). Persuasiveness and persuasibility as related to intelligence and extraversion. *British Journal of Social and Clinical Psychology*, 4: 17.

Caspi, A. *et al.* (2003). Influence of life stress on depression: Moderation by a polymorphism of the 5-HTT gene. *Science*, 301: 386–9.

Cattell, R. B. (1943). The description of personality: Basic traits resolved into clusters. *Journal of Abnormal and Social Psychology*, 38: 476–506.

——— (1965). *The Scientific Analysis of Personality* (London: Penguin).

Cavedini, P. *et al.* (2002). Frontal lobe dysfunction in pathological gambling. *Biological Psychiatry*, 51: 334–41.

Chen, C. *et al.* (1999). Population migration and the variation of dopamine D4 receptor (DRD4) allele frequencies around the world. *Evolution and Human Behavior*, 20: 309–24.

Chotai, J. *et al.* (2002). The temperament scale of novelty seeking in adolescents shows an association with season of birth opposite to that in adults. *Psychiatry Research*, 111: 45–54.

Chotai, J. *et al.* (2003). Variation in personality traits in adolescents and adults according to their season of birth: Further evidence. *Personality and Individual Differences*, 35: 897–908.

Claridge, G. (ed.) (1997). *Schizotypy: Implications for Illness and Health*, (Oxford: Oxford University Press).

_____ and Davis, C. (2001). What's the use of Neuroticism? *Personality and Individual Differences*, 31: 383–400.

_____ Pryor, R., and Watkins, G. (1990). *Sounds from the Bell Jar: Ten Psychotic Authors* (London: Macmillan).

Cohen, L. *et al.* (1999). A man who borrowed cars. *The Lancet*, 353: 54.

Coid, J. *et al.* (2006). Prevalence and correlates of personality disorder in Britain. *British Journal of Psychiatry*, 188: 423–31.

Costa, P. T. and McCrae, R. R. (1980). Influence of extraversion and neuroticism on subjective well-being: Happy and unhappy people. *Journal of Personality and Social Psychology*, 38: 668–78.

_____ _____ (1992). Four ways five factors are basic. *Personality and Individual Differences*, 135: 653–65.

_____ _____ (1993). Bullish on personality psychology. *The Psychologist*, 6: 302–3.

_____ _____ and Arenberg, D. (1980). Enduring dispositions in adult males. *Journal of Personality and Social Psychology*, 38: 793–800.

_____ _____ and Holland, J. L. (1984). Personality and vocational interests in an adult sample. *Journal of Applied Psychology*, 69: 390–400.

_____ _____ and Kay, G. G. (1995). Persons, places and personality: Career assessment using the Revised NEO Personality Inventory. *Journal of Career Assessment*, 3: 123–39.

_____ Terraciano, A., and McCrae, R. (2001). Gender differences in personality traits across cultures: Robust and surprising findings. *Journal of Personality and Social Psychology*, 81: 322–31.

Cravchik, A. and Goldman, D. (2000). Neurochemical individuality: Genetic diversity among human dopamine and serotonin receptors and transporters. *Archives of General Psychiatry*, 57: 1105–14.

Daly, M. and Wilson, M. (1985). Child abuse and other risks of not living with both parents. *Ethology and Sociobiology*, 6: 196–210.

Depue, R. A. and Collins, P. F. (1999). Neurobiology of the structure of personality: Dopamine, facilitation of incentive motivation, and extraversion. *Behavioral and Brain Sciences*, 22: 491–520.

——— *et al.* (1994). Dopamine and the structure of personality: Relation of agonist-induced dopamine activity to positive emotionality. *Journal of Personality and Social Psychology*, 67: 495–8.

DeYoung, C. G., Peterson, J. B., and Higgins, D. M. (2005). Sources of Openness/Intellect: Cognitive and neuropsychological correlates of the fifth factor of personality. *Journal of Personality*, 73: 825–58.

Diener, E. and Emmons, R. A. (1985). The independence of positive and negative affect. *Journal of Personality and Social Psychology*, 50: 1031–8.

——— Larsen, R. J., and Emmons, R. A. (1984). Person x situation interactions: Choice of situations and congruence response models. *Journal of Personality and Social Psychology*, 47: 580–92.

Digman, J. M. (1990). Personality structure: Emergence of the five-factor model. *Annual Review of Psychology*, 50: 116–23.

——— (1997). Higher-order factors of the Big Five. *Journal of Personality and Social Psychology*, 73: 1246–56.

Ding, Y. -C. *et al.* (2002). Evidence of positive selection acting at the human dopamine receptor D4 gene locus. *Proceedings of the National Academy of Sciences*, 99: 309–14.

Dingemanse, N. J. *et al.* (2002). Repeatability and heritability of exploratory behaviour in great tits from the wild. *Animal Behaviour*, 64: 929–38.

——— ——— (2003). Natal dispersal and personalities in great tits (Parus major). *Proceedings of the Royal Society, B* 270: 741–7.

——— ——— (2004). Fitness consequences of avian personalities in a fluctuating environment. *Proceedings of the Royal Society, B* 271: 847–52.

Dobson, K. and Franche, R. L. (1989). A conceptual and empirical review of the depressive realism hypothesis. *Canadian Journal of Behavioural Science*, 21: 419–33.

Dolan, M. and Fullam, R. (2004). Theory of mind and mentalizing ability in antisocial personality disorders with and without psychopathy. *Psychological Medicine*, 34: 1093–102.

Dugatkin, L. A. (1992). Tendency to inspect predators predicts mortality risk in the guppy, Poecilia reticulata. *Behavioral Ecology*, 3: 124–7.

Dunbar, R. I. M. (1996). *Gossip, Grooming and the Evolution of Language* (London: Faber).

Ebstein, R. P. (2006). The molecular genetic architecture of human personality: Beyond self-report questionnaires. *Molecular Psychiatry*, 11: 427–45.

——— et al. (1996). Dopamine D4 receptor Exon III polymorphism associated with human personality trait of sensation-seeking. *Nature Genetics*, 12: 78–80.

Egan, S. and Stelmack, R. M. (2003). A personality profile of Everest climbers. *Personality and Individual Differences*, 34: 1491–4.

Eisenberger, N. I., Lieberman, M. D., and Williams, K. D. (2003). Does rejection hurt? An fMRI study of social exclusion. *Science*, 302: 290–2.

Ernst, C. and Angst, J. (1983). *Birth Order: Its Influence on Personality* (Berlin: Springer-Verlag).

Eysenck, H. J. (1967). *The Biological Basis of Personality* (Springfield, IL: Thomas).

———(1970). *The Structure of Human Personality* 3rd edn. (London: Methuen).

Eysenck, M. W. (1997). *Anxiety and Cognition: A Unified Theory* (Hove: Psychology Press).

Faith, M. S. et al. (2001). Gender differences in the relationship between personality dimensions and relative body weight. *Obesity Research*, 9: 647–50.

Fehr, E. and Fischbacher, U. (2003). The nature of human altruism. *Nature*, 425: 785–91.

Fink, B. et al. (2005). Facial symmetry and the 'big-five' personality factors. *Personality and Individual Differences*, 39: 523–9.

Fisher, R. A. (1930). *The Genetical Theory of Natural Selection* (Oxford: Clarendon Press).

Fiske, D. W. (1949). Consistency of the factorial structures of personality ratings from different sources. *Journal of Abnormal and Social Psychology*, 44: 329–44.

Fleeson, W. (2001). Toward a structure- and process-integrated view of personality: Traits as density distributions of states. *Journal of Personality and Social Psychology*, 80: 1011–27.

Frank, R. H. (1999). *Luxury Fever: Why Money Fails to Satisfy in an Era of Excess* (New York: Free Press).

Friedman, H. S. *et al.* (1993). Does childhood personality predict longevity? *Journal of Personality and Social Psychology*, 65: 176–85.

—— (1995). Psychosocial and behavioural predictors of longevity: The aging and death of the 'Termites'. *American Psychologist*, 50: 69–78.

Furnham, A. and Heaven, P. (1999). *Personality and Social Behaviour* (London: Arnold).

Galton, F. (1884). The measurement of character. *Fortnightly Review*, 36: 179–85.

—— (1885). The measurement of fidget. *Nature*, 32: 174–5.

Gilbert, P. (1997). *Overcoming Depression: A Self-Help Guide Using Cognitive Behavioural Techniques* (London: Robinson).

Giros, B. *et al.* (1996). Hyperlocomotion and indifference to cocaine and amphetamine in mice lacking the dopamine transporter. *Nature*, 379: 606–12.

Goldberg, L. R. (1990). An alternative 'description of personality': The Big-Five factor structure. *Journal of Personality and Social Psychology*, 59: 1216–29.

—— *et al.* (2006). The International Personality Item Pool and the future of public-domain personality measures. *Journal of Research in Personality*, 40: 84–96.

Gosling, S. D. (2001). From mice to men: What can we learn about personality from animal research? *Psychological Bulletin*, 127: 45–86.

—— and John, O. P. (1999). Personality dimensions in non-human animals: A cross-species review. *Current Directions in Psychological Science*, 8: 69–75.

—— Rentfrow, P. J., and Swann, W. B. (2003). A very brief measure of the Big-Five personality domains. *Journal of Research in Personality*, 37: 504–28.

Gow, A. J. *et al.* (2005). Goldberg's IPIP five-factor markers: Internal consistency and concurrent validity in Scotland. *Personality and Individual Difference*, 39: 317–29.

Grant, J. W. G. and Baylys, I. A. E. (1981). Predator induction of crests in morphs of the *Daphnia carinata* King complex. *Limnology and Oceanography*, 26: 201–18.

Grant, P. (1986). *Ecology and Evolution of Darwin's Finches* (Princeton, NJ: Princeton University Press).

Green, M. J. and Williams, L. M. (1999). Schizotypy and creativity as effects of reduced cognitive inhibition. *Personality and Individual Differences*, 27: 263–76.

Gross, J. J., Sutton, S. K., and Ketelaar, T. (1998). Relations between affect and personality: Support for the affect-level and affective-reactivity views. *Personality and Social Psychology Bulletin*, 24: 279–88.

Gross, M. T. (1991). Evolution of alternative reproductive strategies: Frequency-dependent sexual selection in male bluegill sunfish. *Philosophical Transaction of the Royal Society*, 332: 59–66.

Gurrera, R. J. *et al.* (2005). The five-factor model in schizotypal personality disorder. *Schizophrenia Research*, 80: 243–51.

Halushka, M. K. *et al.* (1999). Patterns of single-nucleotide polymorphism at candidate genes for blood-pressure homeostasis. *Nature Genetics*, 22: 239–47.

Hariri, A. R. *et al.* (2002). A susceptibility gene for affective disorders and the response of the human amygdala. *Science*, 297: 400–3.

_____ (2005). 5-HTTLPR polymorphism impacts human cingulate-amygdala interactions: A genetic susceptibility mechanism for depression. *Archives of General Psychiatry*, 62: 146–52.

Harris, J. R. (1998). *The Nurture Assumption: Why Children Turn Out the Way They Do* (New York: The Free Press).

_____ (2006). *No Two Alike: Human Nature and Human Individuality*, (New York: Norton).

Harpur, T. J., Hart, S. D., and Hare, R. D. (1994). Personality of the psychopath. In P. T. Costa and T. A. Widiger (eds.), *Personality Disorders and the Five-Factor Model of Personality*, (Washington, DC: American Psychological Association), 149–74.

Hart, S. D. and Hare, R. D. (1996). Psychopathy and antisocial personality disorder. *Current Opinion in Psychiatry*, 9: 129–32.

Hartman, P., Reuter, M., and Nyborg, H. (2006). The relationship between date of birth and individual differences in personality and general intelligence: A large-scale study. *Personality and Individual Differences*, 40: 1349–62.

Haselton, M. G. and Miller, G. F. (2006). Women's fertility across the cycle increases the short-term attractiveness of creative intelligence compared to wealth. *Human Nature*, 17: 50–73.

Headey, B. and Wearing, A. (1989). Personality, life events and subjective well-being: Towards a dynamic equilibrium model. *Journal of Personality and Social Psychology*, 57: 731–9.

Healey, M. D. and Ellis, B. J. (2007). Birth order, conscientiousness and openness to experience. Tests of the family-niche model of personality using a within-family methodology. *Evolution and Human Behavior*, 28: 55–9.

Hermans, E. J., Putman, P., and Honk, J. van (2006). Testosterone administration reduces empathetic behavior: A facial mimicry study. *Psychoneuroendocrinology*, 31: 859–66.

Horn, N. R. *et al.* (2003). Response inhibition and impulsivity: An fMRI study. *Neuropsychologia*, 41: 1959–66.

Ishikawa, S. S. *et al.* (2001). Increased height and bulk in antisocial personality disorder and its subtypes. *Psychiatry Research*, 105: 211–19.

Jamison, K. R. (1989). Mood disorders and patterns of creativity in British writers and artists. *Psychiatry*, 32: 125–34.

Jang, K. L., Livesley, W. J., and Vernon, P. A. (1996). Heritability of the Big Five personality dimensions and their facets: A twin study. *Journal of Personality*, 64: 577–91.

—— *et al.* (1998). Heritability of facet-level traits in a cross-cultural twin sample: Support for a hierarchical model of personality. *Journal of Personality and Social Psychology*, 74: 1556–75.

Jefferson, T., Herbst, J. H., and McCrae, R. R. (1998). Associations between birth order and personality traits: Evidence from self-reports and observer ratings. *Journal of Research in Personality*, 32: 498–509.

Jennions, M. D., Moller, A. P., and Petrie, M. (2001). Sexually selected traits and adult survival: A meta-analysis. *Quarterly Review of Biology*, 76: 3–36.

Jensen, K. *et al.* (2006). What's in it for me? Self-regard precludes altruism and spite in chimpanzees. *Proceedings of the Royal Society, B* 273: 1013–21.

John, O. P. (1990). The 'Big Five' factor taxonomy: Dimensions of personality in natural language and questionnaires. In L. A. Pervin (ed.), *Handbook of Personality Psychology: Theory and Research* (New York: Guilford Press), 66–100.

——— Angleitner A., and Ostendorf, F. (1988). The lexical approach to personality: A historical review of trait taxonomic research. *European Journal of Personality*, 2: 171–203.

Johnson, D. P. (2004). *Overconfidence and War: The Havoc and Glory of Positive Illusions*, (Harvard: Harvard University Press).

Johnson, G. R. (2000). Science, Sulloway, and birth order: An ordeal and an assessment. *Politics and the Life Sciences*, 19: 211–45.

Johnson, W. *et al.* (2004). Marriage and personality: A genetic analysis. *Journal of Personality and Social Psychology*, 86: 285–94.

Joinson, C. and Nettle, D. (2005). Season of birth variation in sensation seeking in an adult population. *Personality and Individual Differences*, 38: 859–70.

Jung, C. G. (1921). *Psychological Types* (New York: Harcourt Brace).

Keefe, J. A. and Magaro, P. A. (1980). Creativity and schizophrenia: An equivalence of cognitive processes. *Journal of Abnormal Psychology*, 89: 390–8.

Keller, M. C. and Miller, G. F. (2006). Resolving the paradox of common, harmful heritable mental disorders: Which evolutionary genetic models work best? *Behavioral and Brain Sciences*, 29: 385–452.

Kelly, E. L. and Conley, J. J. (1987). Personality and compatibility: A prospective analysis of marital stability and marital satisfaction. *Journal of Personality and Social Psychology*, 52: 27–40.

Kenrick, D. T. and Funder, D. C. (1988). Profiting from controversy: Lessons from the person-situation debate. *American Psychologist*, 43: 23–34.

King, L. A., Walker, L. M. and Broyles, S. J. (1996). Creativity and the five-factor model. *Journal of Research in Personality*, 30: 189–203.

Kinderman, P., Dunbar, R. I. M., and Bentall, R. P. (1998). Theory-of-mind deficits and causal attributions. *British Journal of Psychology*, 89: 191–204.

Knutson, B. *et al.* (2001). Anticipation of increasing monetary reward selectively recruits nucleus accumbens. *Journal of Neuroscience*, 21: 1–5.

Kraaykamp, G. and Ejick, K. van (2005). Personality, media preferences, and cultural participation. *Personality and Individual Differences*, 38: 1675–88.

Krueger, R. F. (1999). The structure of common mental disorders. *Archives of General Psychiatry*, 56: 921–6.

Larsen, R. J. and Ketelaar, T. (1989). Extraversion, neuroticism and susceptibility to positive and negative mood induction procedures. *Personality and Individual Differences*, 10: 1221–8.

—— —— (1991). Personality and susceptibility to positive and negative affective states. *Journal of Personality and Social Psychology*, 61: 132–40.

Lesch, K.-P. *et al.* (1996). Association of anxiety-related traits with a polymorphism in the serotonin transporter gene regulatory region. *Science*, 274: 1527–31.

Liddle, B. and Nettle, D. (2006). Higher-order theory of mind and social competence in school age children. *Journal of Cultural and Evolutionary Psychology*, 4: 231–46.

Lilenfeld, L. R. R. *et al.* (2006). Eating disorders and personality: A methodological and empirical review. *Clinical Psychology Review*, 26: 299–320.

Livesley, A. J. *et al.* (1998). Phenotypic and genetic structure of traits delineating personality disorder. *Archives of General Psychiatry*, 55: 941–8.

Lubman, D. I., Yücel, M., and Pantelis, C. (2004). Addiction, a condition of compulsive behaviour? Neuroimaging and neuropsychological evidence of inhibitory dysregulation. *Addiction*, 99: 1491–502.

Ludwig, A. (1995). *The Price of Greatness: Resolving the Madness and Genius Controversy* (New York: Guilford Press).

Lummaa, V. *et al.* (1998). Seasonality of births in *Homo sapiens* in pre-industrial Finland: Maximisation of offspring survivorship. *Journal of Evolutionary Biology*, 11: 147–57.

Lynam, D. R. *et al.* (2005). Adolescent psychopathy and the big five: Results from two samples. *Journal of Abnormal Child Psychology*, 33: 431–43.

McAdams, D. P. (1996). Personality, modernity and the storied self: A contemporary framework for studying persons. *Psychological Inquiry*, 7: 295–321.

—— (1999). Personal narratives and the life story. In L. A. Pervin and O. P. John (eds.), *Handbook of Personality*, 2nd edn. (New York: Guilford Press), 478–500.

McCrae, R. R. (1987). Creativity, divergent thinking and Openness to Experience. *Journal of Personality and Social Psychology*, 52: 81–90.

—— and Costa, P. T. (1989). Reinterpreting the Myers-Briggs Type Indicator from the perspective of the five-factor model of personality. *Journal of Personality*, 57: 17–40.

—— —— (1997). Conceptions and correlates of Openness to Experience. In R. Hogan, J. Johnson, and S. Briggs (eds.), *Handbook of Personality Psychology* (San Diego: Academic Press), 826–48.

—— —— (2003). *Personality in Adulthood: A Five-Factor Theory Perspective*, 2nd edn. (New York: Guilford Press).

MacDonald, K. (1995). Evolution, the 5-Factor Model, and Levels of Personality. *Journal of Personality*, 63: 525–67.

McGue, M. and Lykken, D. T. (1992). Genetic influence on risk of divorce. *Psychological Science*, 3: 368–73.

McKenzie, J., Taghavi-Khonsary, M., and Tindell, G. (2000). Neuroticism and academic achievement: the Furneaux Factor as a measure of academic rigour. *Personality and Individual Differences*, 29: 3–11.

McQuaid, J. R. and Carmona, P. E. (2004). *Peaceful Mind: Using Mindfulness and Cognitive Behavioral Psychology to Overcome Depression* (Oakland: New Harbinger Publications).

Magnus, K., Diener, E., Fujita, F., and Pavot, W. (1993). Extraversion and neuroticism as predictors of objective life events: A longitudinal analysis. *Journal of Personality and Social Psychology*, 65: 1046–53.

Matthews, G. *et al.* (2002). Personality variable differences between disease clusters. *European Journal of Personality*, 16: 1–21.

Maynard-Smith, J. (1982). *Evolution and the Theory of Games* (Cambridge: Cambridge University Press).

Mealey, L. (1995). The sociobiology of sociopathy: An integrated evolutionary model. *Behavioral and Brain Sciences*, 18: 523–99.

Meier, B. P. and Robinson, M. D. (2004). Does quick to blame mean quick to anger? The role of agreeableness in dissociating blame and anger. *Personality and Social Psychology Bulletin*, 30: 856–67.

Michalski, R. L. and Shackleford, T. K. (2002). An attempted replication of the relationships between birth order and personality. *Journal of Research in Personality*, 36: 182–8.

Miles, B. (1989). *Ginsberg: A Biography* (London: Viking).

Miller, G. F. (2000). *The Mating Mind: How Mate Choice Shaped the Evolution of Human Nature* (London: Heinemann and New York: Doubleday).

Mischel, W. (1968). *Personality and Assessment* (New York: Wiley).

——— and Shoda, Y. (1998). Reconciling processing dynamics and personality dispositions. *Annual Review of Psychology*, 49: 229–58.

Mithen, S. (1999). *The Prehistory of the Mind: The Cognitive Origins of Art, Religion and Science* (London: Thames & Hudson).

Mohr, C. *et al.* (2001). Loose but normal: A semantic association study. *Journal of Psycholinguistic Research*, 30: 475–83.

Montague, P. R. and Berns, G. (2002). Neural economics and the biological substrates of valuation. *Neuron*, 36: 265–84.

Morag, M. *et al.* (1999). Psychological variables as predictors of rubella antibody titers and fatigue: A prospective, double-blind study. *Journal of Psychiatric Research*, 33: 389–95.

Moutafi, J., Furnham, A., and Paltiel, L. (2005). Can personality factors predict intelligence? *Personality and Individual Differences*, 38: 1021–33.

Munafò, M. R. *et al.* (2003). Genetic polymorphisms and personality in healthy adults: A systematic review and meta-analysis. *Molecular Psychiatry*, 8: 471–84.

Nesse, R. M. (1991). What good is feeling bad? The evolutionary utility of psychic pain. *The Sciences*, Nov/Dec: 30–7.

_____ (2000). Is depression an adaptation? *Archives of General Psychiatry*, 57: 14–20.

_____ (2005). Natural selection and the regulation of defensive responses. *Evolution and Human Behavior*, 26: 88–105.

Nettle, D. (2001). *Strong Imagination: Madness, Creativity and Human Nature* (Oxford: Oxford University Press).

_____ (2002). Women's height, reproductive success and the evolution of sexual dimorphism in modern humans. *Proceedings of the Royal Society*, B 269: 1919–23.

_____ (2004a). Evolutionary origins of depression: A review and reformulation. *Journal of Affective Disorders*, 81: 91–102.

_____ (2004b). Adaptive illusions: Optimism, control and human rationality. In D. Evans and P. Cruse (eds.), *Emotion, Evolution and Rationality* (Oxford: Oxford University Press), 191–206.

_____ (2005a). An evolutionary approach to the extraversion continuum. *Evolution and Human Behavior*, 26: 363–73.

_____ (2005b). *Happiness: The Science behind your Smile* (Oxford: Oxford University Press).

_____ (2006a). The evolution of personality variation in humans and other animals. *American Psychologist*, 61: 622–31.

_____ (2006b). Language: Costs and benefits of a specialised system for social information transmission. In J. Wells (ed.). *Social Information Transmission and Human Biology* (London: Taylor & Francis), 137–52.

_____ (2006c). Schizotypy and mental health amongst poets, visual artists and mathematicians. *Journal of Research in Personality*, 40: 876–90.

_____ (2007). Empathizing and systemizing: What are they, and what do they contribute to our understanding of psychological sex differences? *British Journal of Psychology*, 98: 237–55.

_____ and H. Clegg (2006). Schizotypy, creativity and mating success in humans. *Proceedings of the Royal Society*, B 273: 611–15.

_____ _____ (2007). Personality, mating strategies, and mating intelligence. In G. Geher and G. F. Miller (eds.), *Mating Intelligence*. Mahwah, NJ: Erlbaum.

———and Liddle, B. (2007). Agreeableness and theory of mind: Two empirical studies. Manuscript: Newcastle University.

Nigg, J. T. *et al.* (2002). Big five dimensions and ADHD symptoms: Links between personality traits and clinical symptoms. *Journal of Personality and Social Psychology*, 83: 451–69.

Nolen-Hoeksema, S. (2007). *Abnormal Psychology*, 4th edn. (New York: McGraw Hill).

Norman, W. T. (1963). Toward an adequate taxonomy of personality attributes: Replicated factor structure in peer nomination personality ratings. *Journal of Abnormal and Social Psychology*, 66: 574–83.

Omura, K., Constable, R. T., and Canli, T. (2005). Amygdala gray matter concentration is associated with Extraversion and Neuroticism. *Neuroreport*, 16: 1905–8.

O'Steen, S., Cullum, A. J., and Bennett, A. F. (2002). Rapid evolution of escape ability in Trinidadian guppies (Poecilia reticulata). *Evolution*, 56: 776–84.

Parker, W. D. (1998). Birth order effects in the academically talented. *Gifted Child Quarterly*, 42: 29–38.

Patin, V. *et al.* (2005). Effects of prenatal stress on anxiety and social interactions in adult rats. *Developmental Brain Research*, 160: 265–74.

Paulhus, D. L., Trapnell, P. D., and Chen, D. (1999). Birth order effects on personality and achievement within families. *Psychological Science*, 10: 482–8.

Pelaez-Nogueras, M. *et al.* (1994). Infants of depressed mothers show less 'depressed' behavior with their nursery teachers. *Infant Mental Health Journal*, 15: 358–67.

Pembrey, M. E. *et al.* (2006). Sex-specific, male-line transgenerational responses in humans. *European Journal of Human Genetics*, 14: 159–66.

Pennebaker, J. W. and King, L. A. (1999). Linguistic styles: Language use as an individual difference. *Journal of Personality and Social Psychology*, 77: 1296–312.

Penner, L. A. *et al.* (2005). Prosocial behaviour: Multilevel perspectives. *Annual Review of Psychology*, 56: 365–92.

Persico, N., Postlethwaite, A., and Silverman, D. (2004). The effect of adolescent experience on labor market outcomes: The case of height. *Journal of Political Economy*, 112: 1019–53.

Pervin, L. A. (ed.) (1990). *Handbook, of Personality Psychology: Theory and Research* (New York: Guilford Press).

_____ and John, O. P. (eds.) (1999). *Handbook of Personality Psychology: Theory and Research.*, 2nd edn. (New York: Guilford Press).

Peterson, J. B. and Carson S. (2000). Latent inhibition and Openness in a high-achieving student population. *Personality and Individual Differences*, 28: 323–32.

Petrie, M. (1994). Improved growth and survival of offspring of peacocks with more elaborate trains. *Nature*, 371: 598–9.

Phillips, H. (2006). Just can't get enough. *New Scientist*, 26 August: 30–5.

Pickering, A. D. and Gray, J. A. (1999). The neuroscience of personality. In L. A. Pervin and O. P. John (eds.), *Handbook of Personality Psychology: Theory and Research.*, 2nd edn. (New York: Guilford Press), 277–99.

Plomin, R., Asbury, K., and Dunn, J. (2001). Why are children in the same family so different? Nonshared environment a decade later. *Canadian Journal of Psychiatry*, 46: 225–33.

_____ and Daniels, D. (1987). Why are children in the same family so different from each other? *Behavioral and Brain Sciences*, 10: 1–16.

Pound, N. (2006). Facial symmetry predicts personality. Paper presented at the 18th Human Behavior and Evolution Society Conference, Philadelphia.

Prokosch, M. D., Yeo, R. A., and Miller, G. F. (2005). Intelligence tests with higher g-loadings show higher correlations with body symmetry: Evidence for a general fitness factor mediated by developmental stability. *Intelligence*, 33: 203–13.

Rammstedt, B. and John, O. P. (2007). Measuring personality in one minute or less: A 10-item short version of the Big Five inventory in English and German. *Journal of Research in Personality*, 41: 203–12.

Rawlings, D. and Freeman, J. L. (1997). Measuring paranoia/suspiciousness. In G. Claridge (ed.), *Schizotypy: Implications for Illness and Health* (Oxford: Oxford University Press), 38–60.

Retz, W. *et al.* (2004). Psychometric and psychopathological characterization of young male prison inmates with and without attention
deficit/hyperactivity disorder. *European Archives of Psychiatry and
Clinical Neuroscience*, 254: 201–8.

Rhodes, G., Simmons, L. W., and Peters, M. (2005). Attractiveness
and sexual behaviour: Does attractiveness enhance mating success?
Evolution and Human Behavior, 26: 186–201.

Rodgers, B. and Pryor, J. (1998). *Divorce and Separation: The Outcomes for
Children* (York: Joseph Rowntree Foundation).

Saudino, K. J. *et al.* (1997). Can personality explain genetic influences on
life events? *Journal of Personality and Social Psychology*, 72: 196–206.

Schultz, W. *et al.* (1992). Neuronal activity in monkey ventral striatum
related to the expectation of reward. *Journal of Neuroscience*, 12:
4595–610.

Silk, J. B. *et al.* (2005). Chimpanzees are indifferent to the welfare of
unrelated group members. *Nature*, 437: 1357–9.

Slutske, W. S. *et al.* (2005). Personality and problem gambling: A
prospective study of a birth cohort of young adults. *Archives of General
Psychiatry*, 62: 769–75.

Soldz, S. and Vaillant, G. E. (1999). The big five personality traits and
the life course: A 45-year longitudinal study. *Journal of Research in
Personality*, 33: 208–32.

Stiller, J. and Dunbar, R. I. M. (2007). Perspective-taking and social
network size in humans. *Social Networks*, 29: 93–104.

Sulloway, F. J. (1996). *Born to Rebel: Birth Order, Family Dynamics and
Creative Lives* (New York: Pantheon).

Swendsen, J. D. *et al.* (2002). Are personality traits familial risk factors for
substance use disorders? Results of a controlled family study. *American
Journal of Psychiatry*, 159: 1760–6.

Taylor, S. E. and Brown, J. D. (1992). Illusion and well-being: A social
psychological perspective on mental health. *Psychological Bulletin*, 103:
193–201.

―――― and Gollwitzer, P. M. (1995). Effects of mindset on positive illusions.
Journal of Personality and Social Psychology, 69: 213–26.

Taylor, S. E. *et al.* (2000). Biobehavioral responses to stress in females: Tend-and-befriend, not fight-or-flight. *Psychological Review*, 107: 411–29.

Thurstone, L. L. (1934). The vectors of mind. *Psychological Review*, 41: 1–32.

Tokar, D. M., Fischer, A. R., and Subich, L. M. (1998). Personality and vocational behavior: A selective review of the literature, 1993–7. *Journal of Vocational Behavior*, 53: 115–53.

Tooby, J. and Cosmides, L. (1990). On the universality of human nature and the uniqueness of the individual: The role of genetics and adaptation. *Journal of Personality*, 58: 17–67.

——— ——— (1992). The psychological foundations of culture. In J. Barkow, L. Cosmides, and J. Tooby (eds.), *The Adapted Mind: Evolutionary Psychology and the Generation of Culture* (New York: Oxford University Press), 19–136.

Townsend, F. (2000). Birth order and rebelliousness: Reconstructing the research in Born To Rebel. *Politics and the Life Sciences*, 19: 135–56.

Troisi, A. (2005). The concept of alternative strategies and its relevance to psychiatry and clinical psychology. *Neuroscience and Biobehavioral Reviews*, 29: 159–68.

Tupes, E. C. and Christal, R. C. (1961). Recurrent personality factors based on trait ratings. Originally a USAF technical report, this work was republished in 1992, *Journal of Personality*, 60: 225–51.

Turkheimer, E. and Waldron, M. (2000). Nonshared environment: A theoretical, methodological, and quantitative review. *Psychological Bulletin*, 126: 78–108.

Volkow, N. D. and Fowler, J. S. (2000). Addiction, a disease of compulsion and drive: Involvement of orbitofrontal cortex. *Cerebral Cortex*, 10: 318–25.

Völlm, B. A. *et al.* (2006). Neuronal correlates of theory of mind and empathy: A functional magnetic resonance imaging study in a non-verbal task. *Neuroimage*, 29: 90–8.

Watson, D. and Clark, L. A. (1988). Positive and negative affectivity and their relation to anxiety and depressive disorders. *Journal of Abnormal Psychology*, 97: 346–53.

———— ——(1997). Extraversion and its positive emotional core. In R. Hogan, J. Johnson, and S. Briggs (eds.), *Handbook of Personality Psychology* (San Diego: Academic Press), 767–93.

——Gamez, W., and Simms, L. J. (2005). Basic dimensions of temperament and their relation to anxiety and depression: A symptom-based perspective. *Journal of Research in Personality*, 39: 46–66.

Watson, P. J. and Andrews, P. W. (2002). Towards a revised evolutionary analysis of depression: The social navigation hypothesis. *Journal of Affective Disorders*, 71: 1–14.

Whittle, S., Allen, N. B., Lubman, D. I., and Yücel, M. (2006). The neurobiological basis of temperament: Towards a better understanding of psychopathology. *Neuroscience and Biobehavioral Reviews*, 30: 511–25.

Widiger, T. A. *et al.* (1994). A description of the DSM-III-R and DSM-IV personality disorders within the five-factor model of personality. In P. T. Costa and T. A. Widiger (eds.), *Personality Disorders and the Five-Factor Model of Personality* (Washington, DC: American Psychological Association), 41–58.

Wilde, O. (1973). *De Profundis and Other Writings* (London: Penguin.)

Wilkowski, B. M., Robinson, M. D., and Meier, B. P. (2006). Agreeableness and the prolonged spatial processing of prosocial and antisocial information. *Journal of Research in Personality*, 40: 1152–68.

Wimmer, H. and Perner, J. (1983). Beliefs about beliefs: Representation and constraining function of wrong beliefs in young children's understanding of deception. *Cognition*, 13: 103–28.

Zhou, Q. -Y. and Palmiter, R. D. (1995). Dopamine-deficient mice are severely hypoactive, adipsic and aphagic. *Cell*, 83: 1197–209.

Zimmerer, E. J. and Kallman, K. D. (1989). Genetic basis for alternative reproductive tactics in the pygmy swordtail, *Xiphophorus nigrensis*. *Evolution*, 43: 1298–307.

Index